GROUND
SWELL

ADVANCE PRAISE

"Scott Martin has thought long and hard about why waves are so important in the order of things. He understands the power of their energy and how that energy can be harnessed. As any surfer or sailor will tell you, it's more fun to ride a wave than to be rolled by one, and Martin understands that, too."

—**Susan Casey**, author of *The Wave: In Pursuit of the Rogues, Freaks, and Giants of the Ocean*

"Like the great Wayfinders who navigated the vast Pacific, Scott Martin is a navigator for these times. His book masterfully demonstrates the subtle and profound interplay between Nature and business. For anyone seeking greater advancement and meaning in their lives and professions, Groundswell is a must-read!"

—**Dr. Elizabeth Lindsay**, National Geographic Explorer

"Windswells are waves made by the wind—all on the surface and not very reliable. That's traditional brand marketing. Groundswells come from the core of the ocean, carry forward for hundreds of miles, and are rock solid in their delivery. That's the kind of brand marketing Scott is talking about. Why would you want anything else?"

Geoffrey Moore, author of *Crossing the Chasm* and *Zone to Win*

"A powerful approach to doing more while feeling better, Groundswell is chock full of motivational and practical advice for every entrepreneur."

—**Jay Baer**, marketing and CX expert and co-author of *Talk Triggers*

"Over the past twenty years, I have seen Scott apply our ideas, principles, and frameworks in his work with clients, and he recently became one of our Certified Experience Economy Experts. His integration of this thinking into Groundswell—both his business and this book—will cause a new wave of transformative experiences. It's a wave you will not want to miss."

—**B. Joseph Pine II**, co-author of *The Experience Economy: Competing for Customer Time, Attention, and Money*

"Scott Martin is a rare and gifted marketer. In his latest book, he brilliantly argues that brands must strive for more than short-term gains and that their leaders must infuse more of their own humanity into their work. In addition to making a strong business case for higher ideals, Scott also offers his readers clear and pragmatic guidelines for growing sustainably with style. Groundswell underscores brands that stage elegant and aesthetic experiences in the customer journey that transform from typically forgetful to uniquely remarkable."

—**Pauline Brown**, founder and President of Aesthetic Intelligence Labs and Former Chairman of LVMH North America

"You could just start a regular, old business. Or, you could start a movement that makes a real impact on the lives of others while living out your dreams and passions. Sounds better, right? Much better. This book will be your guide."

—**Joe Pulizzi**, author of six bestselling books including *Content Inc.* and *Epic Content Marketing*

"After spending the last thirty-plus years building a business through strategic partnerships, I view Scott Martin and his methods in this book to be absolutely on target. Because you are reading this book, you *are already in a growth mindset. Now go and implement everything here and see what happens."*

—**Brian Bradley**, VP Brand Development at Egoscue

"In the case of human living, a groundswell comes from the invisible inertia found in everything. It then builds momentum from the surrounding inclinations and inferences—which are also often invisible—to arrive at a position of incredible power to deliver. When you apply this to your modern world of achievement—whether in professional, or personal life—you come to understand how essential it is to have this awareness of life's invisible inertias surrounded by countless angles of inclination and inference. This is the awareness that builds your wave of success to its maximum levels. Scott Martin's intuitive awareness of the physics of marketing, waves, and groundswell—as displayed on the pages of this book—is why this form of guidance becomes vital to anyone wanting to succeed in their life personally, professionally, and socially. This gives you the authority to intelligently 'go for it'—without timidity."

—**Guru Singh**, CEO Kundalini University

"I've been fortunate to see how Scott gets stories from his podcast guests, but now reading his own story and framework for growth is both relatable and motivating. A great read for business leaders looking to create a wave and bring people along."

—**Randy Frisch**, author of *F#ck Content Marketing: Focus on Content Experience to Drive Demand, Revenue & Relationships*

"In Groundswell, *surfer, marketer, and entrepreneur Scott Martin brilliantly connects the power of waves to the idea that radical empathy*

and a focus on people can drive profitable growth. This is a must-read for anyone weary of the status quo and ready to make a change, however small, to start building a groundswell."

—**Michael Brenner**, author of *Mean People Suck*

"There are many books out there about marketing who claim they bring something new—they do not; it's the same old, same old, parcelled up with a big red bow on it. With Groundswell, *Scott* writes about marketing but in the age of digital, internet and social media. This is now just what the modern buyer expects of a business today, but he explains how to build a business to market to that buyer from the ground up."

—**Timothy Hughes**, author of *Social Selling* and *Smarketing*

"Today's entrepreneurs seem obsessed with creating businesses that get to cash flow as quickly as possible, always with a focus on the exit door. Scott reminds us that the PROCESS of creating cash flows from ideas is what needs to be carefully created in order to be able to repeat success. Within his carefully crafted book and podcasts, inspiration and lessons from others are shared with a friendly and encouraging tone that will help organize the process for even the most seasoned entrepreneur."

—**Jeff Pensiero**, co-founder of Baldface Lodge

"Scott's outlook on life and business is refreshing. The ability to create a sustainable business that feeds your soul—that's the dream we are all chasing, and building our own groundswell is the path to achieve that dream!"

—**Gary Henderson**, author of *The Clubhouse Creator*

"This book provides a blueprint for any creator exploring how to create a community with impact and a sustainable business at the same time. The surfing metaphor of a groundswell is perfect for building a movement. If you're searching for a contemporary approach to create an independent and important brand this book is for you."

—**Gina Bianchini**, CEO and co-founder of Mighty Networks

"Scott Martin is a powerhouse with deep knowledge in marketing and branding focused on sustainability, organic growth, and integrity. For those of us who run purpose-driven businesses and care deeply about building companies congruent with our values and doing good for our employees and customers alike, Scott shows us how to create a marketing groundswell consistent with our mission. What I have learned by working with Scott has been invaluable, and I encourage any small business leader to read this book and learn from Scott. In a world where impatient growth can be commonplace, Scott charts a unique path with Groundswell. This refreshing book leans into patient and healthy growth specifically applicable to benevolent brands aiming to do good."

—**Jake Wood**, keynote speaker, author of *Once A Warrior*, and founder of Team Rubicon and Groundswell

"Scott's upbringing in a home committed to community service and respect for the planet provides the background for his development into one of the most important voices of this industry which is undergoing violent disruption as we speak.

New technology has enabled thousands of creators to engage markets in ways never thought possible by legacy marketing and media firms. Scott brings the knowledge of those traditional practices to compliment his intuitive approach to new platforms and strategies for building successful brands.

The branding and communications work that Scott has done in my own company has created momentum and resilience that rivals much bigger and longer standing organizations both in and out of my industry. His combined use of traditional and completely untested methods has left my market both intrigued and compelled to participate.

Groundswell is the long-anticipated articulation of Scott's passion for his work. The unique approach he takes to building campaigns and practices that generate inertia reflect his genuine commitment to helping both humanity and the planet. In this book he lays out the overlapping and reinforcing principles that he has taught me over the years that we have worked together. As you move through each chapter you will gain the insights necessary to create an impact in both your market and your community—profitably and responsibly.

This groundswell started long ago and far away, and now it is in reach. Let's paddle in."

—**Mitch Hancock**, founder of Basecamp

"Scott's methodology enables brands to pull their clients in through shared values rather than pushing them away with interruption marketing. The four-step process of Build, Give, Grow, Transform is the potent solution we have all been looking for to market with respect and ultimately get the results we need to share our messages.

Simply put, Scott's strategy helps mission-driven founders to create the wealth and impact they desire. Anyone craving a new and more successful way to market should stop what they are doing—and paddle in."

—**Katrina Wyckoff**, founder of Vertica Fitness

"Scott has launched and built our brand and marketing strategies at both Mod Financial and Mod Jets. This book is the playbook for companies like us that who are looking to make an impact helping others and generating the next modern wave of business growth."

—**Andre Vicario**, founder of Mod Jets and Mod Financial

"After running my company for over thirty years and feeling a disconnection with my direction and overall mission, I worked with Scott to rebrand and merge three companies. I never could have never imagined the depth of connection Scott had with nature and how that directly related to the principles he is teaching with these marketing models. Now I am excited again about the possibilities within my business and the depth of connection I feel with my clients, our community, and with the work that we do. This book is not a marketing fad but a purpose-driven movement to light up this world!"

—**Matthew Sadler**, founder of Rutsu

"The tide is rising for forward-thinking brands to implement empathetic, human-centric cultures. Scott's framework in Groundswell underscores this to be critical for sustainable growth, today and into the future."

—**Jenn Lim**, author of *Beyond Happiness*

THE UNSEEN WAVE OF
BUSINESS GROWTH

GROUND SWELL

SCOTT A. MARTIN

LIONCREST
PUBLISHING

Groundswell

The Unseen Wave of Business Growth

ISBN 978-1-5445-3935-5 Hardcover
      978-1-5445-3936-2 Paperback
      978-1-5445-3937-9 Ebook

Illustrations by Taylor Kinser
Groundswell Sketch by Fabian Lavater
Cover Photo by Morgan Maassen

TO MY JILLYFISH

CONTENTS

FOREWORD xvii

PADDLE OUT *(a Note from the Author)* xxi

ORIGINS

WAVES OF HIDDEN POTENTIAL 3

THE GROWTH DILEMMA 25

A CONTEMPORARY VISION FOR GROWTH 41

FINDING YOUR EPIC ORIGINS 59

BUILD

PATIENCE IS THE NEW GROWTH HACK. 73

A NOTE ABOUT AUTHENTICITY. 111

CONNECTION IS THE NEW CASH 117

PLAYING THE LONG GAME. 155

WAVES UPON WAVES 189

GET GIVE

GIVE IS THE NEW GET 197

WHEN GIVING LEADS TO GETTING. 241

GROW

GROUNDSWELL IS THE NEW GROWTH 255

PATIENCE IS STILL THE NEW GROWTH HACK 299

TRANSFORM

BEYOND LOYALTY. 307

THE SEA OF SAMENESS 329

ACKNOWLEDGMENTS. 339

ABOUT THE AUTHOR. 345

FOREWORD

Across the more than twenty years since I first met Scott Martin, our conversations have always revolved around one simple truth that we take to be self-evident: individual human beings are at the core of every company's reason for being.

Over that same period of time, it has been pretty safe to say that very few companies operate as though they accept that truth. Far too many companies behave in a manner that dehumanizes the people around them. The terms we use to describe these people include customers, employees, vendors, and community members. But those terms often enable—rather than slow—this dehumanization process.

No one wakes up in the morning and says, "I can't wait to assume my role as a customer of Acme Corporation." No one.

Instead, we wake up and think: I'm hungry…I should go to the diner for breakfast. Or perhaps: my sweater is looking a little ratty; maybe I should order a new one. By the same token, very few executives wake up and think: time to make my employees miserable today.

To varying degrees, most of us are victimized by a system that over numerous decades has become exceptionally buggy. It emphasizes short-term results so strongly that long-term results suffer. It causes leaders to unintentionally demotivate employees, often until that same system turns against the leaders and causes them to lose their jobs. It frustrates the people who are spending their hard-earned money ("customers"), who often opt for the least-bad of numerous disappointing options.

Who is the villain in this story?

All of us.

The villain isn't out there. Every single one of us who accepts the status quo is to blame. Every one of us who says, "That's just the way the system works," is making it possible for the system to keep working that way (i.e., very badly).

In this book, Scott Martin makes the case that there is a much better alternative. We can and should run businesses in a manner that treats individuals—and the natural environment around us—with deep respect. Importantly, that includes you, whether you are a founder, a president, an investor, or the newest intern on the block.

Doing business in a more humane manner also means treating yourself with respect and honoring the ways that you work best.

Scott has long divided his time well between business, adventure, and life. He doesn't see the ocean and mountains as separate from work life. He recognizes that each of us lives our entire lifetime in a very thin strip of air, tight against this planet's surface. No matter how much time you spend in an air-conditioned office, you are part of the natural ecosystem of this planet, and your interests are bound tightly together with the rest of ours.

Let's join together and form a Groundswell that elevates every human being. Let's treat ourselves and others with respect. When we spot a dehumanizing belief, process, or practice, let's call it out and fix it.

We are not powerless; we are all-powerful. Together, we can build a much better way to get stuff done. Instead of complaining, let's give the business world a major upgrade.

Together, let's build a Groundswell!

Bruce Kasanoff
Park City, Utah

PADDLE OUT

(a Note from the Author)

I first want to thank you for picking up this book and taking the time to invest in looking at business differently. The tide is rising for forward-thinking founders, discerning entrepreneurs, and brave brands who desire sustainable growth marketing.

This new approach I call Groundswelling—a powerful, yet currently unseen wave of elegant business growth—is actually not that new. I have just identified the patterns and modelled them into a framework that helps impact creators and entrepreneurs who crave building something that lasts.

How to read this book: I encourage you to consider reading it one of two ways.

- Find a chapter or section that catches your eye and jump right in. I have broken them down into concepts that can stand on their own if you're looking for something specific. If you don't know just open the book use your intuition (like pulling a deck of cards) pick a page. Make a note of the page and share in our community of other readers what ideas or synergies came up after reading. groundswelling.com
- Read like you're starting a journey to thinking differently. Allow the book to be pondered and enjoyed cover to cover. There are five sections: Origins, Build, Give, Grow, and Transform.

Origins is the why and the backstory that gives the entire book context. It will help you understand the foundation, as well as the changes affecting business that lead to the reference to Groundswell as a wave/movement—and its application to building a sustainable-growth business.

Build is where I explain the profound benefits of starting your process with strategic planning, active strategy, and building demand. Many will want to skip to the Grow section; but without Build, you have limited growth.

Give is the secret sauce. It's the start to building momentum and generating initial growth to meet the changing business landscape.

This section teaches how to shift from chasing attention to getting buy-in and meeting the evolving attitudes of your audience.

Grow is likely the biggest reason you picked up this book. It's my hope that this section will be a reference guide you'll revisit and reread. Use it to hold your team or stakeholders to a new standard and to transform typical growth into transformative growth.

Transform explains the ultimate growth loop—how to go beyond loyalty and create exponential growth while decreasing energy and costs over time. This section covers the three phases of delivery to master Groundswelling and transform your business growth.

The common theme across each section is simply a journey toward business sovereignty, going from dependency on traditional costly marketing methods to independence and elegant growth.

ORIGINS

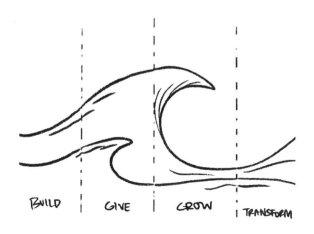

BUILD | GIVE | GROW | TRANSFORM

WAVES OF HIDDEN POTENTIAL

"I'm just a surfer who wanted to build something that would allow me to surf longer."

—Jack O'Neill, inventor of the wet suit

Surfers, like entrepreneurs, are passionate about catching their next dream wave. And entrepreneurs, like surfers, possess a clear vision of the future they seek—but they're often at the mercy of their environment when it comes to bringing that vision to fruition.

We know we want to ride a wave, but the waves are hard to catch and can be temperamental.

In surfing, the most common of these temperamental waves are called wind swells. Generated by nearby storms, wind swells are fickler and less powerful than the waves called groundswells. As a surfer, you typically ride wind swells and waves that are coming from several directions, and tempo and length can be fragmented.

The more desirable waves, called groundswells, are bigger swells from a larger storm farther away. These waves are generated by distant storms with enough force to penetrate to the ocean floor. The initial result of storms is a chaotic spectacle of waves flowing out from the epicenter, in every direction across the ocean. As they move, groundswell waves combine their energy and transform into unified lines, flowing forward like a parade of well-trained foot soldiers marching in the same direction. From above, they're long, clean parallel lines resembling an old pair of corduroys until they finally reach the shallowing ocean floor, breaking their smooth tops into beautiful white crests. Each crest of a groundswell outlasts that of a wind swell, and when it finally touches down in the impact zone, the spectacle isn't over. Row after row of beautiful lines move toward shore, changing into cresting waves and seemingly endlessly transforming into breaking waves.

I had the chance to meet over Zoom with the amazing Susan Casey, author of *The Wave: In Pursuit of the Rogues, Freaks, and Giants of the Ocean*, and afterward she shared with me her definition of *groundswell*:

> A groundswell is born from the ocean's energy, and it reaches far and deep. It's a steamrolling lump of power that's destined to travel, and along the way it organizes itself. It is steady and inexorable. It can be counted on to deliver upon its promise.

These legendary waves are a surfer's dream, and to experience them requires lucky timing. It's difficult to predict when a groundswell will take place. This famous Instinct ad from the 1980s captures the longing of a surfer's heart: "Waiting for waves is okay. Most people spend their lives waiting for nothing."

I had the extraordinary opportunity to interview the founder of Instinct, world champion surfer Shaun Tomson, on my podcast. He shared that this brand campaign was aimed to be authentic, with his marketing creating a connection to surfers based on a deep understanding of their intimate relationship to surfing and the waves.

In the past, our longing for waves could only be fulfilled by waiting, sometimes paddling out in flat surf in hopes that a sneaker wave would roll in, or endlessly staring at the horizon. If you live where the water is cold, like it is in most great surf destinations, waiting for waves can be very chilly.

I can't imagine surfing for any length of time, let alone paddling out, prior to the invention of the wet suit. It must have been the ultimate frustration to go into freezing water—or, worse, to watch waves roll in, unridden due to the water temperature.

But lucky for us all, the world has changed.

When avid surfer Jack O'Neill invented the neoprene wet suit that allowed him to surf during the cold California winters, he had set out to create something useful for himself—to scratch his own itch, so to speak. But he accomplished so much more. He created meaning and fulfillment for his entire surfing community, which gave him the freedom to follow his dreams and transform the surfing world forever.

Over the years, as progress allowed for the modernization of travel, forecasting tools, and on-demand technology, surfers gained more agency than ever before. We no longer had to wait and hope for more waves or warmer water, or even wait for the mystical groundswell to appear. Instead, we could identify, scout, and pinpoint groundswells' origins in the vast ocean—see them coming. We could travel and meet them.

It doesn't stop there. Now, the world has changed again; and surfers no longer have to wait for waves at all; we can create our own.

In 2017, world champion surfer Kelly Slater joined Adam Fincham, surfer and engineering specialist in geophysical fluid dynamics, and a team from USC Viterbi School of Engineering, to launch a feasibility study for a surf pool that would create perfect waves a surfer could ride indefinitely.

Fast-forward to 2020. Using the science of waves, Kelly Slater's Surf Ranch is the world's most advanced "wave generator" wave pool. It manufactures waves that mimic those of a perfect, never-ending groundswell. Not only are they considered physically perfect, but these waves will also soon be made with fully sustainable energy by harnessing solar power.

After his first ride on one of Kelly's waves, surfing legend Gerry Lopez said, "That's the future, bro."

The longing of the surfer is the same as the longing of the entrepreneur—to paddle into a wave of our dreams.

And for me, both surfer and entrepreneur, seeing the resounding impact of the passionate focus of Jack and those who followed in his footsteps changed the way I look at entrepreneurship and marketing forever.

THE BIG O

My unique story began literally at birth: I was adopted. My loving adoptive parents jokingly said to me that I was "literally picked," unlike my other four siblings. As a middle child, it's clear my primary motivator was, "How do I stand out and make a difference?" In retrospect, it's no surprise that I landed in marketing. Or that my connection to marketing came from my love of surfing, despite growing up landlocked in Canada.

My first trip to the ocean was when I was around four years old. My parents had taken us to Hawaii. I remember the smell of coconut, the salty taste of the sea, the roll of the waves at my feet, and just feeling…awestruck. When I was nine, my entrepreneurial parents left the trappings of an indoor pool and ranch in Canada to volunteer around the world. Our first move was to southern California, where my introduction to the power of connecting brand and belonging came from surf and skate culture. Our house was near a local skatepark called The Big O, which was down the street from the original Van's shoe shop, where you could get your shoes custom made to order. It was the coolest. On my tenth birthday, a friend gave me a T-shirt from The Big O. It became the most worn shirt in my personal history, infamous for its holes; I wore it until it literally disintegrated. It was so much more than a shirt. Why? It was different than my Vans shoes, Op shorts, and Lightning Bolt tees. The Big O shirt was more authentic—real to me, local to me, like I was part of an inner circle.

MY LIGHTNING BOLT

Then, when I was eleven, we moved to the Philippines so my parents could volunteer on a more permanent basis. My little brother and I had the ultimate jungle story adventures, complete with a pet monkey named Chico. I'd pour over the surfer magazines I had brought with me, but I had yet to stand up on a board myself. After living there for some time, we got the chance to spend a week at the ocean. I was incredibly excited. My father and I built a wooden hollow surfboard, painted completely red and decorated with a big yellow lightning bolt, just like the board in pictures of the amazing Hawaiian surfer Gerry Lopez dropping into North Shore's pipeline.

We moved back to Canada when I was in junior high. I faithfully wore my Vans, Hawaiian shirts, and surf wear, which made me stand out like a palm tree in an igloo. The hockey players and headbangers harassed me, but a small group of the most attractive girls in school gave me the opposite attention. Not such a bad trade. I became obsessed with my dream to move to the North Shore to surf and windsurf—so much so that I spent most of my class time in high school doodling drawings of waves. When I could finally drive, my buddy Jamie and I would skip class and load up my VW van with windsurfing gear and head out to the local lake.

I ended up short by one credit and didn't finish high school, but I did save enough money to move to the North Shore of Maui shortly after my would-be graduation. I lived there for over a year, surfing and windsurfing to my heart's content. It was everything I thought it would be, for a while. Eventually, I became weary of being a Canadian working under the table; though I was rich with the surfing lifestyle, I was relatively broke financially. Even after I returned to Calgary, my longing for the ocean was so strong that I would travel back to Maui and spend winter with the waves.

EMBARKING ON ENTREPRENEURSHIP

Throughout my entire journey, I had started a multitude of little businesses, stoking the fires of my entrepreneurial heart. Van's shoe shop led to my obsession with personalization technologies and mass customization of goods, as well as marketing and branding. The Big O T-shirt was branded in my mind and the first of many experiences that connected me to the power of being part of something that was bigger than just commerce.

Along with spending as many hours as I could in the ocean, my other constant pursuit was reading as much as possible—anything and everything I could get my hands on about business and marketing. By the time I was in my early twenties, I was smack dab at the forefront of the Internet's growth and got to put my knowledge to good use.

I was fortunate enough to land a job with a fast-growing startup selling websites. I impressed the CEO, Cameron Chell, who was also a venture capitalist, and he funded and mentored me as the founder and CEO of a new internet startup called Next Click: The Personalization Agency. During this burgeoning growth period of the Internet and digital marketing, lightning struck: I got a front-row seat and was flat-out obsessed with learning about how personalization and one-to-one strategies could humanize marketing, simultaneously lowering costs and increasing sales and loyalty.

Let me take one step back and share how my lightning bolt moment came—on one meaningful, sublime, and fateful day.

MAKING PERSONAL IMPACT

One day, my entire outlook on business changed forever. I went to an event where a speaker named Don Peppers was keynoting and sharing the insights from a just-released book he'd coauthored with Dr. Martha Rogers, *Enterprise One to One*. He shared the impacts of personalization and how you can build an unparalleled experience with these technologies and strategies. The lightning strike of ideas and possibilities had me running up to meet Don and have him sign my book. I don't remember what I said, or even what he said, but I know how I felt: stoked. There was a new, deep knowledge in me that this was going to change how brands market, and I could be part of it.

This knowledge led to an obsession with learning, reading anything I could get my hands on about the topic—which included a book by my other mentor, Joe Pine, called *Mass Customization*. Both Joe and Don shaped the trajectory of my entire career in marketing. I co-founded The Personalization Consortium with Don and Dr. Martha Rogers, aimed at furthering innovation in the industry while self-regulating with standards aimed at ethical information management around personally identifiable details. We had an impressive board of directors from American Airlines, KPMG, Price Waterhouse Coopers, Double Click, United Airlines, and many others. Both Don and Martha were leading the industry with making impact personal and with good ethics. I was just grateful that they collaborated on the vision.

It was during this time that I met Bruce Kasanoff and was honored to be asked to write a comment for his book *Making It Personal: How to Profit from Personalization without Invading Privacy*.

I deeply admire Bruce Kasanoff and his poignant perspective about business: the only way to do great business is by building connections and relationships with our fellow humans. He advocates for looking at people—customers, clients, employees—as humans first. This stands in stark contrast to the mainstream marketing landscape that turns people into targets. Instead, to grow your business well, you must embrace radical empathy for your fellow humans. Design your business to be human, and treat others as human, first and foremost.[1] Because only when business and growth are intertwined with personal purpose can it be truly *meaningful*—a critical measure of success.[2]

Groundswells are all about being a force for good. Principles like radical empathy; deeper relationships; and commitment to helping others move, change, and transform are the bedrocks of this sustainable-growth model.

If this sounds like you, you're in the right place. Read on.

I have had the immense privilege of sitting down with the aforementioned top minds in business, as well as many others, to talk about the incoming next wave of business and marketing strategies for brands of impact. My guests are amazingly generous with their unique points of view on my central topic: Sustainable Growth Marketing. I am beyond grateful for their support during the process of writing this book over three seasons and almost seventy episodes. I will be sharing their insights throughout.

---

[1]   Scott A. Martin, "Scott Martin | Introduction to Groundswell Marketing," March 8, 2019, in *Groundswell Origins*, podcast, 52:03, https://groundswell origins.com/podcast/scott-martin.

[2]   Bruce Kasanoff, *Making It Personal: How to Profit from Personalization without Invading Privacy* (New York: Basic Books, 2001).

These "Captains of Industry" have been charting the choppy waters of a rapidly dynamic and sometimes inclement environment and directly leading the way for brands to market ethically and effectively. You are here to uncover the unseen so you can build better, faster, and more meaningfully.

AMBITIOUSLY LAZY

It's my hope that you'll connect with me and recognize there's a more elegant way to do business—a way that is meaningful, sustainable, and makes a positive impact. This has been a personal obsession—how to sustainably build and grow a brand of impact and keep customers coming back. I have developed a personal philosophy that has led to a way of thinking I call being "ambitiously lazy." Translation? How can I essentially do more with less? This book is, at its essence, about how *you* can exponentially grow sustainably with less costs or effort over time while also making a positive impact on humans and the world we live in.

My obsession with applying this approach began when I launched my first marketing agency and has continued to this day. I worked for over twenty-five years in branding, marketing, and strategy with national brands like Best Buy, Detroit Pistons, WestJet, Travel Alberta, Calgary Flames, Forzani Group, Hudson's Bay Company, and many more. I then shifted in the last decade to a narrower focus on brands of impact, working with founders, creators, and marketers who are looking for uncommon results but still using common sense. This is how I started seeing patterns in my own experience and identifying patterns in other brands around sustainable business growth.

My mission is to help other entrepreneurs unlock this unique hidden potential within their business. And I've written this book just for us.

DIG DEEP AND PADDLE OUT

The ocean has been my biggest
teacher, and I have been assiduously
studying patterns to see
if there is a connection
between the unques-
tionable success of
sustainable growth in
nature and business.

At a Business Mastery
event I attended, Tony
Robbins shared his strat-
egy for successful brands:
"You first identify patterns, then
differentiate patterns, and then create
new patterns." This is the methodology of my deep-dive into
this thinking.

I have identified, differentiated, and created new growth strategies (patterns) modeled after nature, as well as studied both
business and my own personal experience. This approach has
uncovered a truth from brands across multiple industries
and sizes: all growth is not the same, just as all waves are not
the same.

The cycles of nature offer ubiquitous models we can look to for clarity and inspiration for how growth happens. A seed, for example, is planted and nourished until it sprouts and then grows until it produces its own seeds. In water, energy starts as a ripple and grows to a swell until it nears the shore, at which point it breaks, forming the white-crested waves that crash over the reef with powerful impact. A groundswell begins not as a ripple, but as an impressive storm. The waves are disparate. It is only when they unify and collaborate, forming bigger waves together, that their power truly begins to grow, wave upon wave. This epic start to the storm ends in an Epic Outcome when it reaches its destination on the coast.

Whether a seed or a wave, growth occurs as a natural phenomenon, forming under specific conditions and taking on particular characteristics. In either case, the outcome we seek is not immediate. It begins small and must develop in sequence, over time. But it is this model from nature that we can mindfully pursue across our organizations, businesses, and personal lives to achieve the sustainable growth and impact we desire to experience and share with others.

Whether you're a business owner or a marketer, it's time to reimagine your mindsets and practices related to growth marketing. Give yourself permission to question the way things have always been done. Join the ranks of passionate entrepreneurs who, like Jack

O'Neill and Kelly Slater, dared to do something no one had seen before. Learn how to start a Groundswell and make an impact that spreads far and wide in the sphere you care about most deeply.

This book is intended to be a guide, roadmap, and reference for impact-driven entrepreneurs, conscious creators, and mindful and maverick marketers who crave this kind of meaningful and sustainable long-term growth. Tapping into your hidden wave of marketing potential will ensure that you build sustainable growth for years to come, which will allow you to do more of what you love and make a more meaningful impact on what matters most to you.

My aims for you when you complete this book are vital for creating a Groundswell:

- Recognize where there is economic waste, and activities that aren't aligned with your core values and don't lead to growth sustainability.
- Stop directing ineffective energy toward growing your business with traditional marketing that is aimed at interrupting humans, and shift instead to energy that captivates, magnetizes, and builds trust with your audience.
- Start doing things that align with your values—and harness the endless energy that will grow your connection to your brand, your audience, and your outcomes.

- Understand the profound value of addressing your audience as humans—not customers—as unique individuals in every moment.
- Take the time to Build; then begin your efforts with a Give before you focus on Growing.
- Start building momentum with Giving as a strategy.
- Generate a movement that creates change and ultimately guides your audience into waves of Transformation.
- Ask yourself in every interaction: is this sustainable, is it human-centric, and does it help move, change, and transform the world to become better?

Over time, Groundswelling becomes ingrained in the totality of your business—it is an outward expression and demonstration of what your business is.

To build a Groundswell, you simply must lead with your heart.

It's time to be brave, dig deep, and paddle out.

THE GROWTH DILEMMA

"If you're not growing, you're dying."

—Tony Robbins

The traditional benchmark of business success is growth. Sales, customers, profits, and increased likes, subscribers, and so forth— these are the traditional metrics that feed the hungry appetite of growth, and so businesses do whatever is necessary to keep these numbers climbing. But can they sustainably continue to grow?

Thanks to the Internet and digital platforms, the world is more connected than ever before, creating more opportunity to get in front of your chosen audience—but competition for attention is fierce. Opportunity for you is also opportunity for everyone else. The typical way to stay relevant (and therefore afloat) is through aggressive marketing tactics—such as doubling down on digital ad spend to offer inflated incentives that elbow out the competition. It's a marketing arms race.

This is the current marketing climate.

Unfortunately, most businesses that chase growth with aggressive campaigns typically create only a quick temporary uptick in sales. When the campaign is over, sales fall back to baseline. And when measuring success based on numbers alone, this short-term growth spike doesn't tell the whole story. Chasing these growth numbers is the extent of the brand's vision—to grow for growth's sake. The pattern repeats itself, and they simply have the marketing/sales group prepare and launch the next aggressive campaign to generate another spike.

Growth has become such a high priority that a science of innovative testing resulting in rapid growth has emerged; it's called "growth hacking," and I spent many years learning and deploying this methodology via expert guests on my podcast like Sean Ellis, author of *Hacking Growth*.

Like many others, I have been obsessed with growth. It wasn't until later that I identified that the real dilemma is in the *kind* of growth. Not all growth is the same.

Don't get me wrong—growth hacking is a very rational, strategic, intelligent discipline. It is a science and can work wonders, especially if you can impact product design. I established my career leveraging a singular focus of rapid growth. What I am referring to instead is "hack-tics": looking for shortcuts, chasing trends, and chasing opportunities for rapid, immediate growth. There is a missed opportunity in pursuing only immediate growth. We love to play the hero: create an aggressive campaign to unlock massive growth that is as rapidly visible as possible. There was a time when growing *slow* felt like failure because I was obsessed with measuring speed with increased growth numbers. I have to be honest: my actions were extremely short-sighted. I unknowingly, like so many others, was fixating on revenue at the expense of relationships.

Often, we hear stories in the trade publications of brands that deploy the well-known growth tactics and gain a flood of new sales and customer acquisitions. They may appear to be growing, but behind the scenes there tends to be a different story, like customer service failing or operational systems crashing. The influx of growth is overwhelming their infrastructure, which in turn impedes quality service and ultimately damages relationships. So, while they are gaining new customers on the front end, they are simultaneously losing them on the back end. Even if the company is fortunate enough to gain more than they lose, there is little doubt that this growth strategy is not sustainable. And it's all because they can't deliver on their promises long-term.

In fact, it has become clear that not only are the strategies themselves not sustainable, but neither are the marketing channels used to deploy them. Nearly every business today is unknowingly handcuffed to a marketing channel they have become reliant upon that may or may not be around in the future.

The speed of change is remarkable. Remember pop-up ads? Maybe not. Thanks to pop-up blockers, that form of advertising has all but disappeared. Not too long ago we couldn't imagine paying for TV. Now we will gladly pay to opt out of ads, giving rise to commercial-free TV, radio, games, and web pages. How do you market to your audience if you can't advertise? Sharing social posts isn't going to cut it. What happens when the digital platform you've been investing all your marketing efforts in becomes too expensive?

If you're building your entire marketing platform on Facebook or Instagram or Twitter or TikTok, or if your entire store is on Amazon, *they own you.* They can jack up the prices, take a bigger cut, or adjust the algorithm to ensure that no one sees your content unless you pay more. If your strategy only has one lane—if the growth you seek is at the mercy of someone else, another company—and if you're chasing the algorithm, you are sabotaging your potential and sustainability.

I experienced frustration with tyrannical online platforms firsthand. After investing several years into Facebook, I built up a page with sixteen thousand followers. Now I can barely engage organically with my audience on that platform because Facebook requires that I pay to be seen by my own followers. All the energy I spent building that platform was easily exploited by Facebook when they changed the rules. I soon realized that I have little or no control over what happens on these platforms. That experience deepened my resolve to identify and create new ways for brands to diversify and create a sustainable and sovereign capability to grow.

Beyond the challenges of being subject to social platforms' limitations, we need to pay close attention to the changing ecosystems and how audiences voluntarily move. In the digital era, they move fast. I call it cross-channel migration, like a seasonal migration of a herd moving from one area to another. What happens when your audience moves to another channel? What if the channel disappears? Remember MySpace and Google Plus? How will you pivot?

Most brands are scrambling to adapt, get back out front, and stay in proximity to audiences' eyes and ears when this happens. What will this cost you in time, money, and momentum? And what about new businesses? How does a business get off the ground if it can't compete with the huge ad spend of already established companies? Or do they have an advantage?

How many well-meaning brands fail because they build their expectations, business predictions, and infrastructure around a rapid-growth model? And on top of a channel or platform that they don't control?

How many marketing executives get swept away by hype, focusing on amassing followers and subscribers, rather than nurturing relationships?

How many strategists repeatedly invest all their proverbial eggs in platforms they can't control and then, when change inevitably comes, have to start over?

THE TEMPTATION OF RAPID GROWTH

The sweet lure of cookie-cutter, so-called "strategies for exponential, rapid growth" (*and* in a short amount of time) is a seductive trap to fall into. If this sounds familiar to you, or if you've gone down that path, you know how it ends. Typically, not amazing—but not without some learning or some impact. It works, sure; but at what cost?

Rapid growth is incredibly difficult to support, and the magic that leads to that kind of growth tends to be short-lived. Why? You uncovered a trend or opportunity. Nothing wrong with that—being opportunistic is being entrepreneurial. But before you know it, you're addicted to the growth curve and overrun with the pressure to keep up. That's the problem with chasing growth for growth's sake—it is extremely challenging to maintain.

CHASING HACK-TICS

Chasing Mavericks is a movie about a young surfer chasing a dream of surfing northern California's fabled cold big-wave spot called Mavericks. Many of today's brands have marketing departments that are focused only on chasing the one big wave of growth. The problem is that these waves are seasonal, fickle, and hard to catch, aka "short-term events."

Short-term strategies become a treadmill of effort: campaigning for the sales bump again and again and again, only to return to the baseline each time. These shallow efforts typically amount to growth that is short-lived—not true growth, and certainly not sustainable growth. Sometimes you get lucky, but—unfortunately—betting on hacks, tactics, and trending opportunities has become the "whack-a-mole" addiction.

Growing your business too fast without the support in place is dangerously negligent—like a roller coaster that keeps adding cars and passengers without reinforcing the rails and beams.

Some might roll their eyes and argue, "I would love to have the problem of so much growth I don't know what to do with it. Money can just fix that."

Not actually. Pumping in more money without the sustainable strategy just shifts problems. Rapid growth strains your infrastructure until systems fail, which leads to audience expectations going unmet. This lack of fostering strains these vital relationships until you lose them altogether. If you insist on rapid growth before your business is built to handle it, growth itself becomes the underlying cause of death for your business. All the tactics in the world aren't going to fulfill your business goals if you erode trust with the people you serve.

While the opening growth quote by Tony Robbins rings true for most things in life and business, it also applies to tumors. The 10x grow-quick culture that taught us bigger is always better created a malignant tumor in the way most brand marketing departments operate. Not all growth is good. I know this firsthand, as a recovering "fire, ready, aim" 10x rapid-growth marketer. It tends to be unpredictable and unhealthy.

After completing hundreds of hours of training with Tony over the years and attending more than thirty of his events, I know that he is not referring to the bloated, fast, get-rich-quick-at-all-costs kind of growth. He's talking about good, healthy, sustainable growth.

If you single out and focus on top-line growth, you're missing the bigger, more meaningful picture. The dilemma isn't growth itself. It's the type of growth.

© marketoonist.com

THE TRUTH ABOUT GROWTH

In their book *The Long and Short of It*, Peter Field and Les Binet include incredible research on the effectiveness of short-term and long-term strategies across five hundred marketing campaigns. The difference in results demonstrates that short-term sales efforts can generate a seemingly rapid return, but those efforts are not as effective long-term—which is where sustainable growth happens.

The irony of chasing fast growth is that it can tend to lead to short-term growth (i.e., short-termism) but actually, statistically, stunts and impairs *true* growth. Sadly, this sums up the average marketing model—a shallow system that achieves artificial and temporary success.

In surfing, balance is critical. Being off-balance is downright dangerous. The same is true for business. When it comes to the wave of profitability and cash flow, one wrong maneuver and you're wiped out. In fact, learning to balance short-term cash-flow needs and long-term profitability might be one of the most important concepts for business owners, and the marketing teams that support them, to master.

As cartoonist and blogger Tom Fishburne wrote:

Marketing for the long-term and the short-term is a constant balancing act. Pressure to show immediate results can lead marketers to focus on quick-hit sales [conversion] tactics, which can look good temporarily in marketing dashboards, but are far less effective in the long-run… This focus on short-termism [focusing on short-term stopgap measures instead of strategic longer-term activities] is leading marketers astray.[3]

Surrounded by so much noise, panic, and hustle, marketing specialists chase the latest trends and social media algorithms rather than doing what their clients actually need. New platforms pop up promising to be the key to business growth and success—only to die the next day. Old platforms constantly threaten to take you down with an algorithm change. Nothing is more frustrating than seeing your growth held hostage by platforms, tactics, and funnels.

---

[3]   Tom Fishburne, "Marketing Short-Termism," marketoonist, June 10, 2018, https://marketoonist.com/2018/06/short-termism.html; *see also* Tim Koller, James Manyika, and Sree Ramaswamy, "The Case against Corporate Short Termism," *Milken Institute Review*, August 4, 2017, https://www.mckinsey.com /mgi/overview/in-the-news/the-case-against-corporate-short-termism.

TAKES ONE TO KNOW ONE

A lot of things can contribute to rapid growth, but for growth to be *sustainable*, a specific *must-have* foundation has to be in place. I haven't always known what this foundation is. The concept of Groundswelling was born out of failure—my own and that of others.

Now, as a recovering "fire, ready, aim" addict, I know that chasing growth for growth's sake is not the answer. Genuine, healthy growth is not measured by *how much* or *how fast*, but rather by how sustainable it is. When you're thinking about sustainability, you're already thinking about how you will become impervious to change. You plan for what you can do today to secure your future. With that mindset, it is much easier to slow down and do conscientious things ahead of time, rather than having to react from a place of panic.

The best growth—the healthiest and most sustainable growth—ideally happens within infrastructure that strikes a balance between short-term tactics and long-term strategy. But not just any short-term tactics. Building a sustainable brand requires an updated approach to marketing—one that combines common-sense thinking with proven strategies. The kind of marketing that leads to sustainable growth is not just about numbers, likes, shares, and sales. It's about people.

But don't misunderstand—sustainable doesn't require poverty or misery. It doesn't mean poor growth or even slow growth. Sustainable growth includes profit as well as times of rapid growth. Think of it practically: living sustainably doesn't mean you have to live in the woods without power. It's like having a generator or an abundant solar resource. When the system goes down and the power goes out, you're still rolling.

Pursuing sustainable growth does not mean that you shouldn't invest time in the latest digital platforms, like Facebook or TikTok. These and other trends can be tools, but they cannot be the backbone of a sustainable marketing strategy. Instead, *intelligently* invest your time in them, which includes being prepared for them to change. Go in with your eyes wide open. Be sure you're building with value in mind.

With a sustainable growth model, your business has the power to thrive, no matter what the economy is doing.

It's time to abandon the unsustainable pursuit of growth. To stop chasing wind swells or waiting for the perfect storm. Instead, recognize that you have the power to become the storm.

Slow down.

Pause.

Ask yourself: do I simply want to grow bigger and faster—or do I want to grow *better*?

A CONTEMPORARY VISION FOR GROWTH

*"Enlightenment is when a wave
realizes it's the ocean."*

—Thich Nhat Hanh

Think about why you first went into business. Was it just to turn a profit? Was it growth for growth's sake? I highly doubt it. You probably wanted to build something of your own. Something real that matters. Something that will last. This is the heart of the entrepreneur.

It's easy to get lost and to lose sight of what you really want, what really matters to you. The lies that say growing big, growing fast, and selling out are requirements for success—even if deep down you know better—can leave you feeling stuck in a meaningless scramble for profit.

To get back to the heart of your business requires changing the way you think about marketing. It requires an intentional shift from aggressive tactics to positive, value-driven actions. A shift from targeting and acquiring to connecting and serving. This is not just a game of semantics. The words matter. The intent matters. Because the way you make your audience feel matters.

We've all experienced enough advertising that we can smell inauthenticity through our computer screens. Marketing has always been seen as pushy and demanding, for good reason. So much in this world is hollow. It's no wonder people sense when they're being played and instantly reject it. We've made marketing campaigns about what we can get, instead of what *we can give*.

How is your marketing treating people?

How are interruptions at every turn, screaming "Buy, buy, buy!" making them feel?

How is that adding value to their lives?

People are longing for something meaningful they can align with. Instead of being annoyed by your advertisement, they'd prefer to be excited. They *want* to support something that makes them feel invited and able to say, "I am so glad this exists so I can be a part of it."

The current growth-obsessed marketing climate is not serving you or those you serve. The pursuit of growth for growth's sake hijacks your clarity of purpose. It saps your patience and stamina to build something that lasts and shrinks your ability to build relationships and deliver true value. Building genuine relationships of depth and substance is what truly leads to long-term sustainable growth.

Marketing has more power than ever to reach people all across the globe, from every demographic and psychographic. Not only is there opportunity, but there is also a responsibility in the way we interact with the world.

You have a vision and mission—to give value, to serve others, to solve problems, to provide for yourself and your family, to discover innovations, and to see what's possible. Whatever your vision and mission look like, they are important to you, and you want them to last. But you've been told that growth is the only way to make that happen. This concept isn't untrue, but it is incomplete. It's time we all offered our economy and culture a different kind of marketing and growth.

Imagine…a long-term growth strategy that allows you to be relationship-focused rather than transaction-focused—where customers regain their humanity and get to become people again, not just numbers or dollar signs.

Imagine…a focused and strategic plan that is not just one channel, campaign, or funnel, but a diverse ecosystem, founded on the strategic principles, core values, and unique value proposition your brand brings to those you serve.

Imagine…intentionally building momentum and engineering growth through giving—where content and community add value to the lives of your audience without interrupting or selling.

This sustainable approach to marketing and growth is what I now call *Groundswelling*.[4]

---

[4] *Groundswelling* is a name born from Jim Gilmore during a strategy session with me when he was helping me describe "how to build a Groundswell" and what to call the act of doing and building a Groundswell.

WHAT IS SUSTAINABLE GROWTH MARKETING?

Frankly, it's a never-ending journey in business. It's not a destination, it's not a template, and it's evolving. In my view, it is an attitude of searching and adapting to find ways to grow with less effort and economic waste over time, with the aim of exponential growth and outcomes.

I believe it's like an umbrella covering many types of approaches to achieving sustainable growth. It's my view that there will be many future methods and models to look forward to. It's the search for the holy grail of growth.

Currently, three models arise that fit inside this category of being sustainable—*if*, and only if, one very specific attribute is constant and effective: innovation. Without it, none of these models maintains its strength and sustainability.

Word of Mouth: A very traditional and long-standing proven approach is word of mouth. It is very people-centric—people connect with others and share your brand and reputation—and an outstanding way to sustainably grow your business.

Growth Hacking: Growth hacking is an emerging practice involving ongoing marketing experiments and adapting your product offering to be hyper-growth-focused, leveraging word of mouth and creating a "growth loop" where an ongoing system of growth is exponential.

Groundswelling: Groundswelling is extremely purpose-centric; the connection to the product, and every interaction with the brand, is in alignment with your values. This distinction is deeply related to the very word *groundswell* and its two profoundly connected meanings.

BUILD YOUR GROUNDSWELL

First, let's define what a groundswell is.

There is more than one definition of a groundswell.

- the waves created by offshore storms that unify and travel long distances without losing energy
- a grassroots movement, born of a common vision or purpose, that expands to create powerful impact

In both instances, once-rogue individuals join forces with unseen potential and reveal themselves with epic force. Building a foundation of clarity of purpose can galvanize the hearts and minds of your audience, which generates buy-in and momentum in a direction of untold power to grow your brand—this transformation is precisely what creates a Groundswell.

Your business and your audience are more than a trend—they are an ever-flowing tide. When unified, they are capable of generating an ongoing, predictable stream of customers, cash flow, and positive change that will be remembered.

A Groundswell is about moving from selling to sharing.

From guessing to investing.

From capturing to captivating.

From transactions to transformations.

GROUNDSWELLING

The art and science of Groundswelling is the voyage to connect with your audience in a meaningful way that is congruent with your values. This realignment paradoxically shifts you from a position of dependence to one of leverage. When you ask yourself *why—what*, *how*, and *for whom*—your business is growing, you define purpose that is meaningful on a larger scale. This creates an impact for something larger than itself, and only then can the hidden wave of sustainable growth be tapped. In fact, it so thoroughly creates authentic alignment with your ideal audience that the more repugnant aspects of marketing are simply not required.

With Groundswelling, your business focuses on giving value to your audience—more value than they anticipate or expect, followed by even more value. Transformed by their experience with you, your audience is compelled to share with their network, spreading the message of your value far beyond your own reach. As word spreads, your audience grows, and more join with your shared vision of a deeper, more meaningful world.

This shifts your business growth from erratic to predictable—
which, contrary to popular opinion, is actually preferable, even
if it's incremental.

By putting people front and center, a Groundswell creates a
culture of conscious commerce where a business recognizes its
responsibility to add value to the lives of those it serves. This
becomes the heart and soul of your brand and unleashes its hidden potential, exponentially impacting not only the bottom line,
but the world around you for years to come.

ANATOMY OF A GROUNDSWELL

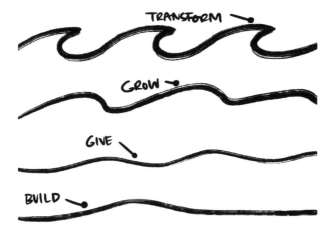

There are four phases of a Groundswell. But I can't explain them without acknowledging the origins of how they were developed. You might remember that Don Peppers (my mentor and marketing master) and Martha Rogers, PhD, wrote a book called *Enterprise One to One*. It is one of the best books I've ever read on marketing. In it, they break down the three keys to marketing: get, grow, keep.

- The first step is simply to acquire *(get)* new customers.
- To *grow* your customer value, you can up-sell more to existing customers or cross-sell other goods or services. Reduce the cost of serving your customers and generate new referrals through word of mouth.

- The three activities that *keep* customers are: retain them longer, win back old customers who have left you, or even eliminate unprofitable customers.

I have used these key principles in every aspect of my career, and they have served me very well, sharpening my approach to client strategies. But over the next two decades after reading *Enterprise One to One*, I made slight revisions in my use of these three principles to accelerate my clients in building a Groundswell.

In that time, I have worked both with national brands and directly with entrepreneurs, applying what I have learned from Don Peppers, Joe Pine, and others. I have evolved and adapted to approach marketing in my own way that is still very much rooted in Don's preeminent work of "get, grow, keep."

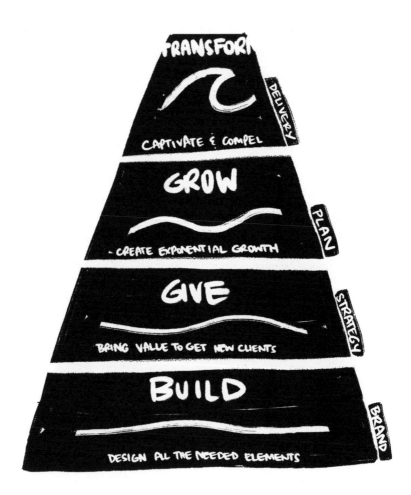

TRANSFORM

Captivate & Compel

DELIVERY

GROW

Create exponential growth

PLAN

GIVE

Bring value to get new clients

STRATEGY

BUILD

Design all the needed elements

BRAND

THE FOUR PHASES OF A GROUNDSWELL

What I identified in my evolution process was a need to place a different emphasis on the relational or good value that would lead to customer acquisition. Instead of focusing so much on how to "get," I began to focus on what I was building that could instill trust in a future customer relationship. In essence, it was my way of taking a step back to think more about my responsibility to the customer rather than thinking about my customer's rationale for trusting me.

What developed from this new perspective was a new ecosystem of sustainable growth—what I identified as the four phases that lead to a Groundswell. Note that these phases build from the ground up.

- Build
- ~~Get~~ Give
- Grow
- ~~Keep~~ Transform

Once initiated, each phase naturally leads to the next. However, no phase ever stops. This rolling progression continues to feed itself, creating self-sustaining growth—the ecosystem of a Groundswell.

These four phases are what we will be discussing in the pages that follow. There will be some direct how-to, but because each

Groundswell endeavor (like each business) has its own unique needs, there is a lot of variability in how to apply it.

The most important aspect at this time is that you understand the spirit and principles behind a Groundswell. This is the ultimate foundation. By applying the principles of a Groundswell to your unique and specific pursuit, you can unlock the unseen wave of hidden potential waiting for you.

A Groundswell Parable:
Origins

To help you generate your own vision for your Groundswell, I'd like to share a story. As much as this is a story of a business, it's a story of two siblings: Koa and Kalani.

Koa started making custom surfboards when he was a teen and specialized in traditional materials and designs. Koa operated on word of mouth, mostly making boards for friends and family. Kalani found a surfboard-making competition for Koa to enter, where the winning board would be chosen and used by a professional surfer. Koa's win really put his talents on the map. After this exciting turn of events, Kalani decided to open an Etsy shop to expand Koa's visibility. Koa worked on boards in the evenings and on weekends, while Kalani processed and shipped orders as well as managed their online presence.

We'll spend the rest of the book tracking their specific problems with growth, as well as their unique Groundswell solutions. This fictional journey will demonstrate what it looks like for two people to align their vision and Build, Give, Grow, and Transform their audience and their business for sustainable growth. It will also help you better see how to make the vision of a Groundswell into your own reality.

For simplicity's sake, we are working with two individuals. Other organizations may have many more stakeholders and decision-makers, but the principles remain the same. As you read about generating a Groundswell in the surfing world, I challenge you to envision your own. How would you break the status quo of traditional growth and service and knock the socks off those you serve?

The parable of the Groundswell Goods Surf Shop is one possible journey to meaningful growth. I dare you to dream up another.

FINDING YOUR EPIC
ORIGINS

*"[The waves] move across a faint horizon,
the rush of love and the surge of grief, the respite
of peace and then fear again, the heart that beats
and then lies still, the rise and fall and rise and fall of
all of it, the incoming and the outgoing, the infinite
procession of life. And the ocean wraps the earth, a
reminder. The mysteries come forward in waves."*

—Susan Casey, *The Wave: In Pursuit of the Rogues,
Freaks, and Giants of the Ocean*

I hope by now it's clear that the days of external marketing, by which you just throw money at someone to buy ad space, are quickly evaporating. Marketing is no longer about getting an ad in front of potential customers so they know that you exist—it's about what you have to say, what you're about, and what you have to offer in the transaction and beyond. For that reason, it is essential to understand the motivation for growth and impact beating at your core. This is your epicenter—or *Epic Center*—where all hidden potential originates.

To have purpose means the things we do are of real value to others. According to *Start with Why* author Simon Sinek, purpose-driven companies attract the best minds, have the most passionate customers, achieve wild success, and change the world. Finding the heart of your purpose is a key process when developing your growth marketing strategy, one that empowers others to buy in without hesitation. Simon Sinek says, "People don't buy *what* you do, they buy *why* you do it. A failure to communicate *why* creates nothing but stress or doubt."

When your values and purpose are congruent and clear, they serve as the rocket fuel for growth. You are able to move with less friction (internally and externally) and focus the greatest amount of energy in the same direction. Just like a Groundswell.

The more important the values you hold, the longer your vision will be—and needs to be. The same holds true for the transformations you want to create and the people you want to impact. Your values, vision, transformation, and impact affect every aspect of your Groundswell endeavor.

You are concentrated at the core like a storm—focused—and, once moving in a unified direction, your invisible energy transforms into visible results like the wind to the waves. You are a gathering storm of good, ready to Build and Give more to the world so you can Grow to have more impact and Transform the world.

FROM EPIC CENTER TO EPIC OUTCOMES

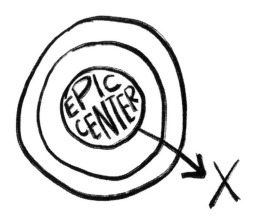

Consider carefully: once you set out from your Epic Center, where is your hidden potential going to lead?

Without disciplined focus, even the most passionate values and vision are not likely to yield transformation and impact—at least not up to their true potential. To generate the congruency of your vision and values—the potential of your Epic Center—you must articulate the specific transformation and impact you want to achieve. You need to put the X on the map, so to speak. That X is a declaration of your *Epic Outcome—your Impact*.

Your Epic Outcome is not just the destination or result you want; it is your North Star—the guiding light that keeps you on course. At any time, you can pause and check in with yourself: Are we heading the right way? Is this taking us closer to or further from our Epic Outcome? What impacts do we want to have?

But how do you know what impacts you want to have and the outcomes they can bring? Aside from business growth objectives, there is another clue to help you find your Epic Impact. It's likely not what you expect. It's not an objective, it's subjective—it's a feeling. What is the feeling you're after when you are trying to achieve your outcomes?

There may be many waves of impact within your outcome. You can impact people in so many ways, and repeatedly, as you aim toward your bigger outcome.

For example: you want to achieve that award because you think it will give you a specific feeling. Perhaps you want to make millions to give you the lifestyle you want, yes—but even that lifestyle is a means to a specific feeling you're after.

Tony Robbins points out that there are countless unhappy millionaires because they thought those millions would make them feel a certain way and then didn't. This leads to disillusionment and a life that feels meaningless.

Finding your Epic Outcome is beginning with the end in mind. What is in your mind in terms of what you want to feel? What impacts do you want your brand to make on the world? What does the impact to your culture look like?

Your clarity may begin at either point, with your Epic Center (motivation to begin) or your Epic Outcome (articulated outcome you want to achieve). But you can leverage one to help you find the other. Knowing why you're beginning can help you find direction, and knowing where you are going allows you to map backward to connect it to your core purpose and motivation. The space in between is where your hidden potential is revealed.

The common theme across each section is simply a journey toward business sovereignty going from dependence on traditional, costly marketing methods to independence and elegant growth.

One thing is clear: there are multiple waves of impact on the journey toward your Epic Outcome.

NOT FOR THE FAINT OF HEART

In 1808, before one of his expeditions to Antarctica, explorer Ernest Shackleton allegedly published this ad in a newspaper:

Men wanted for hazardous journey, small wages, bitter cold, long months of complete darkness, constant danger, safe return doubtful, honor and recognition in case of success.

While a job description like this one may seem like an obvious "hell no" for most, those fierce individuals with a heart for adventure and who value discovery leapt at the chance to be a part of such a trek.

Granted, pursuing a Groundswell may not be as rough as Shackleton's journey, but it will challenge you in ways you can't yet see. Change is always difficult, and we resist it as much and for as long as we can. My hope is that you're already tired of business as usual and ready to discover and build something meaningful.

I have repeatedly heard Tony Robbins share, "Success without fulfillment is the ultimate failure." This book is about building a successful brand *and* having fulfillment—staking your claim on doing something exceptional, hearing the call to go on a journey, and having honor and recognition for impacting the world for the better while you become better. It's about becoming great by doing good.

The elements of building, marketing, and doing business have never been more connected. As we explore the principal elements and life cycle phases of a Groundswell (and the sustainable growth and impact it leads to), you will be required to change more than just the way you market. It's a new way of doing business—I dare say it's a new way to live. A way to fully express the heart and soul of your business, to do business differently from now on and avoid the salty taste of regret over what you could have built.

This is an investment of your time. Think of all steps as an investment, not an expense or a necessary move toward an outcome— it's a journey. Today, many people are unwilling to invest their time, and they wonder why they don't get the results. You need to make the investment of time, effort, and building to get the return on that investment.

To that end, it is important to understand, first and foremost, that creating a Groundswell is not a singular event. It is a process that builds upon itself, creating exponential momentum—one wave at a time. But you shouldn't expect to catch the wave of the latest fad. You shouldn't expect tactics and hack-tics to simply entice people to buy. Instead, roll up your sleeves and prepare yourself for game-changing work that reverberates through every aspect of your business.

The foundation of the Groundswell is not fancy or flashy. It is simultaneously humble and ambitious, compassionate and ruthless, dedicated to a vision and open to change. Like a fluid wave breaking against the ocean floor, these paradoxical dynamics are what give it power. It is on this strange but sturdy ground that you can truly begin to Build.

BYOG:
Build Your Own Groundswell

As you read through each phase of this provocative strategy, I invite you to access the living extension of the book: The Groundswell Blueprint. There you'll find a free downloadable workbook with additional tools, case studies, and access to a community of people sharing their experiences: groundswelling.com/book

BUILD

PATIENCE IS THE NEW GROWTH HACK

PATIENCE IS THE NEW GROWTH HACK

"Patience is bitter, but its fruit is sweet."

—Aristotle

As entrepreneurs and marketers, we are people of action. We're hustlers, willing to do whatever it takes to get the results we are after. This is an admirable trait, but it doesn't always serve us. Rome wasn't built in a day, and neither is a Groundswell. If we want to build something that lasts, we must leverage patience.

The ability to tolerate delay and misfortune without frustration—the sense to stay calm and keep your wits about you when progress slows down—is the essence of patience. In terms of business and marketing, patience is not jumping at the first opportunity for movement or growth, but simply waiting and watching. Then, when the time is right, choose to move with intention. Easy to say, not so easy to execute.

Patience is called virtuous because embodying it isn't easy temporarily, let alone in the long run. Pair the level of difficulty with modern-day business pressures, and it's no wonder (despite their shortcomings) growth hacks are everywhere. How can anyone keep a clear head about long-term vision when they are worried about keeping their business afloat?

Whether it's a cash-flow crisis that threatens making payroll, or fidgety investors looking for short-terms payouts, the pressure is on to perform. This squeezes CEOs and CFOs, who stalk their monthly financials for ways to create some breathing room. The result is often deploying a quick fix that may create a short-term gain but does nothing to help the business in the long run. This is precisely why sustainable growth is so important, and why we need a revised approach.

While things like cash flow and sales goals are real issues a business has to address, a brand pursuing them with tunnel vision misses out on the full potential that is possible. And the price for shortsightedness is too high. As Peter Drucker wrote in *Post-Capitalist Society*, "Long-term results cannot be achieved by piling short-term results on short-term results." Instead, you need to build a foundation you can rely on, and that takes time. It requires discipline, grit, and follow-through. It requires patience.

MINDFULLY PATIENT

"Patience isn't waiting. Patience is knowing."

—Guru Singh

Patience is both a mindset and an action. Said another way, it is an act of mindfulness. Mindfulness, unfortunately, is one of those words that gets thrown around a lot but is seldom understood. Mindfulness is not sitting on a yoga mat in some spaced-out state of mind. Rather, it is the combination of specific, focused *intention* and alert, situational *awareness*.

Let's unpack this treasure.

Intent is the *reason* you take action—the specific result you hope to achieve. You intend to have an impact on your bottom line, the people around you, the market, or the greater world. Intent is your desire to connect your Epic Center to your Epic End.

When it comes to a Groundswell, your intent is so strong that no shiny new object could distract you or detract from it. Knowing and aligning with your intent cultivates patience because you are committed to doing everything you can to achieve the result, even if that means waiting when you can't see the evidence of your intent working. In other words, you gotta have faith.

There are also layers of intent. First is the macro understanding of your Epic Center and your Epic Outcome. This allows you to bring focus to the micro decisions and actions. This alignment of your intent from macro to micro is a direct catalyst for a Groundswell.

When you clearly know *what* you are trying to accomplish, you become aware.

Awareness is observation that leads to understanding. It's knowledge in context: awareness of where you are, where you're going, the obstacles and opportunities that lie in your path, and the actions that are necessary to traverse that path.

True awareness requires intimate knowledge of your intent. Without it, you may be able to observe, but you won't know how to interpret what you see. The context of your intent, both macro and micro, develops situational awareness, which enables you to interpret your present circumstances and adapt intelligently.

When you recognize both the current reality and the future possibilities, you can take right action.

Actions are the methods we use to achieve our intent. When action is aligned with intent and informed by awareness, it is specific, deliberate, and powerful. This is the culmination of mindfulness.

$$\frac{\text{INTENT} + \text{AWARENESS} + \text{ACTION}}{\text{MINDFULNESS}}$$

INTENT + AWARENESS + ACTION = MINDFULNESS

No action is on *accident*; instead, every action is *purposeful*. And after each action, a Groundsweller stays mindful—using awareness to observe the results, then interpreting them according to their intention. Did this action achieve our intended result? Whatever the outcome, looking closely helps wisely determine the next right step.

Patience, it turns out, is ongoing, sustainable mindfulness that leads to ongoing, sustainable growth. Groundswellers aren't waiting around with no good reason, they are actively waiting with intention and awareness, ready to move at a moment's notice. And they understand that Groundswells aren't built with one action, but a cascade of actions that build upon one another. Each action creates motion, generating energy in a specific direction. This energetic motion (e-motion) makes an impact on the micro level, which generates further motion, propelling you forward to create the holy grail of building a Groundswell: momentum. This is the ultimate payoff.

Mindfulness, patience, and momentum are the keys to building growth that lasts—the kind that carries you the distance to your Epic Outcome.

PATIENCE ISN'T PASSIVE

Make no mistake, you do not build a Groundswell by being passive. Instead, you deploy methodical and deliberate execution. World-renowned entrepreneur and author Dean Graziosi, in a podcast interview with me, reminds us that this process is not about getting lucky. It's not hit-a-few-buttons-and-you're-rich. It's a methodical process that first requires the right mindset, followed by the right delivery system, marketing, and product. Not to mention the right ethics and values that make you stand out to your audience—because as you will see in coming chapters, it is ultimately your audience that keeps you going.

This is precisely what we are building in this phase of the Groundswell, but it takes time, and the progress is not always obvious. Patience is active, but that action often occurs beneath the surface. Imagine water building up behind a dam, or a ferocious tiger on the hunt, waiting and watching—the stillness is building up power to be released when the moment is right. In racing—cars, running, speed skating—an athlete may hang back and allow someone else to take the lead. The leader experiences the most wind resistance and has to work harder to stay out front. The athlete knows that it's not about how you start, or even where you are in the pack;

it's about how you finish. So, the athlete moves quickly, but also paces for endurance, patiently watching for the right time to make their move. This strategy of patience expels less energy to get a better result.

Muhammad Ali was the master of patience. To the inexperienced eye he may look like he's not doing much, but he's actually using his patience hack: rope-a-dope. Prior to his famous fight against George Foreman in 1974 in which he used this technique, he was known for going toe-to-toe right from the bell—the equivalent of chasing fast growth. But Ali adjusted his technique, patiently wearing down the younger and heavier-hitting Foreman over the course of the fight, and then went for the knockout. Everybody thought he was losing—until he won.

Patience isn't a crawl, and it isn't a run. It's more like a brisk walk, one that builds the strength and confidence to jog. Then, when timing is ideal, you sprint. But all the while, you know you're running a marathon.

Patience trusts that the process will add up to victory, even if it doesn't look or feel like it in the moment. Case in point: Vanessa Van Edwards.

THE SWAN EFFECT

Vanessa Van Edwards, a top human behavior researcher, author of *Captivate*, and lead investigator at The Science of People, said, "Every business is wearing Spanx to hold in the wobbly stuff."

She is referring to the fact that everyone (including your competitors) looks like they know what they are doing because they hide well what they don't know. We all have wobbly stuff underneath, hidden out of view. To illustrate this idea, she compares business to a swan. On the surface, a swan appears smooth and beautiful, flowing easily above the water. But just below the surface, the swan thrashes in a murky and constant chaotic hustle. The swan is paddling for her life.

I had the privilege of seeing Van Edwards' incredibly moving talk at the World Domination Summit in 2017. She shared the truth about her own swans, the murky depth you don't see, and all the hidden work and time it took for her to achieve her Groundswell. She referred to it as Swan Math.

1. Twitter: ten years of twecting to crack the Twitter code, 3,600 days to find her people, 14,400 tweets to find her voice, and a full-time person behind the scenes.
2. YouTube: nine years of filming to crack the YouTube code, 437 videos to find her people, 2,567 pages of scripts

to find her voice, and numerous people and equipment behind the scenes to make it happen.

3. Blogging: eleven years of blogging, 3,105 posts (not to mention the one thousand unpublished blogs that didn't make the cut), 348 pages of a website.[5]

Today, Van Edwards' website touts the fact that she has done more than a thousand events, spoken to more than fifty thousand attendees, and consulted more than 120 companies. And yet, she started all of this with thirty-four followers. "It's not about finding the most people; it's about finding the *right* people," she said. It took time, but she didn't quit. Instead, she focused on serving, all the while remaining clear and intentional about her outcome.

Rather than making rash decisions and reacting from fear of missing out, stay patient. Do your homework, set your sights, and lay your groundwork until everything is aligned. This prepares you for when the moment of opportunity arrives. When it does, you can strike with authority and confidence. Don't forget to enjoy the climb; and when you're ready, all you have to do is jump.

---

[5] Vanessa Van Edwards, "Motivational Keynote," World Domination Summit, July 2017, YouTube video, 29:01, https://www.youtube.com/watch?v=Cqw JVIMGUHQ&t=37s.

LEADING WITH LONG-TERM VISION

Patience comes more naturally when innovators have a clear and intentional vision, because they know what they're building for. Having this vision and mission at your core invites and encourages people to connect with you in your pursuit and contribute to your Epic Outcome. The depth of this clarity and congruency is key to generating momentum and staying power.

Take the Tesla company, for example. Let's say you were thinking about investing in Tesla when it was founded. From the very start, and still today, you would need to take a long-term view of your investment. Founder Elon Musk made it clear that he intended on disrupting multiple industries, including automotive, electrical, and space travel. These intentions were about a future of goods (products) that were (and are), in some cases, not yet present or proven. But as we flash forward to the time of this writing, both investors and Musk have been rewarded for their patience. It certainly hasn't been without challenges. Musk himself has said, "Patience is a virtue, and I'm learning patience. It's a tough lesson."[6]

Leading requires having the vision *and* the patience to see it through, recognizing that it will be a challenging journey but also widely impactful. Leaders of Groundswells are in the direct position to be a force multiplier for positive change, to create impact that grows and transforms the greater world.

It all begins with you. You are the epicenter of your own Groundswell. And it is your vision that acts as the catalyst for everything you want to build. You don't have to be tossed by the storm—you *are* the storm. You can leverage your own power to make amazing things happen.

---

[6] Phil McKinney, "Patience in Innovation: Success Stories from the Front Lines," philmckinney, September 16, 2016, https://philmckinney.com/patience-in-innovation-success-stories-from-the-front-lines/.

THE BUILDING BLOCKS

To build anything, let alone anything that is meant to last, you need a framework to organize how all the pieces come together. Certainly, that is what Build + Give + Grow + Transform are for your Groundswell. But within each of those phases can be any number of strategies, steps, pieces of content, or infrastructure that are necessary to make your concepts take shape in the real world. Executing your Groundswell-sized vision will require executing smaller-sized visions—and, within those, even smaller visions still. Waves within waves within waves. Use this simple framework to help you envision, break down, and construct your desired outcome for each various layer of your Groundswell.

IDEATE | DIFFERENTIATE | ACTIVATE

Ideate

The first step to your Build blueprint is thinking bigger. Yep, sounds obvious, but as entrepreneur Keith J. Cunningham says in his book *The Road Less Stupid*, "Thinking is critical to sustainable success in business; said another way, business is an intellectual sport."

When you ideate for your Groundswell, think beyond the business as usual.

The ideation phase is all about the quality of thinking and the time you put into thinking about how to maximize your Groundswell and minimize the risk. It all hinges on *thinking time*. Spend serious time thinking about these questions:

- Who can help make this happen?
- What are my potential blind spots?
- How can I keep my options open in case I need to pivot my strategy?

The principles and structure suggested in *The Road Less Stupid* will enable anyone—regardless of size of business, the currency, or the industry—to run their business more effectively, make more money, and dramatically increase the likelihood of keeping that money.

Differentiate

The next step is to take your big vision in ideate and pare down the most potent ideas by differentiating into priorities or separating based on strategic fit. Most people cannot immediately see the overall picture; but if you can articulate the overall vision and then separate "what we are going to do next" into high-level blocked stages, you can contain the plan and give people an achievable vision of what the blueprint is doing in which order.

This step is where you break apart the key elements into a structure so you can communicate and execute what to do in what order.

- First, articulate the aim of the Groundswell—the problems you are solving—and simplify an easy-to-understand outline of your overall plan. What is the focus of your movement, and what is the outcome you aim to have? What Transformation do you want to occur with your audience?
- Separate the phases of your Groundswell so you can break down more modular pieces of your plan for people to digest inside of the Build, Give, Grow, and Transform framework.
- Then, generate a list of priorities, goals, and milestones within each phase; this will allow you to articulate the plan at a level that will help you achieve the milestones.

Activate

Ultimately, the final step to your Build blueprint is to take action— to move from theory into reality.

- The first step feels obvious, but it's key. Start. Do something to verify your plan. Test any aspect of the process of your plan. You actually need to set a time and activity you are going to start on. Take massive but strategic action that gives you some feedback as to the potential audience (customer) response to what you are doing.

- The next action step is to test. What do you need to test to ensure that your planning/thinking and theory are verified? By answering this question, you're effectively dropping that pebble into the ocean so the ripple can turn into a wave. What gets measured gets done, and what gets verified (it's working) becomes the building blocks of what to build upon.

THE PLANNING PARADOX

Taking time in the Build phase to name and strategize your business and marketing is the essential component to shift from wind swell results to a Groundswell. But this doesn't mean you have to know and decide everything before you say the word *go*. It's a balance of the ever-changing dynamics of business evolving and changing.

In the past, before actually taking any action, companies hired marketers to produce vast and intricate marketing plans; but the landscape moves and shifts so fast nowadays that this one-and-done approach is outdated. Even with solid market research, a marketing plan is a hypothesis—a best guess—until it's tested in the field.

Building a Groundswell requires planning and patience, but also agility. Adjusting your plan as you obtain new information is an essential part of the strategy to unlock your full marketing potential. I call this **Active Strategy**.

Active strategy is a live trial balloon that allows you to test a set of assumptions and gauge a response. This can be done on a micro level in a campaign-style activity, like a series of social posts; or it can be done in a more substantial experiment where the posts are part of a larger growth funnel and lead to a landing page that vets a system or a process to determine how much energy and resources it's going to take to pull off. This initial action informs your next action, which is part of planning accordingly.

An example of this kind of experiment is my virtual community. I was looking to test whether I could migrate my thousands of followers in my Facebook and LinkedIn social groups to my private community platform. I did an eight-month beta with my inner circle to figure out how it worked and to identify the patterns of success. Now I can accurately anticipate what it's going to take to Build to scale and what I am going to Give to incentivize users to make the switch. I learned that getting people to switch platforms is hard and that it takes a more compelling Give to incentivize them—which is a fun problem to have and challenges me to get creative.

You don't have to wait until you have everything figured out to act; nor should you jump out so far that you can't adjust course. Both of these extremes have potential drawbacks. How many plans have spun out and never even made it off the ground? Alternatively, how many businesses just got started and decided to figure it out later, only to end up having to start from scratch? Too many, often after experiencing big losses. Instead, the key is to take action concurrently with your planning and research.

Now the marketing plans I build for clients include two types of documentation.

- the traditional business planning documentation that has been used for decades and serves as an anchor point for what you're building—the aspects of your endeavor that are not likely to change (e.g., your Epic Center and your Epic Outcome)
- living documentation that is designed to change, allowing you to utilize contemporary tools to be more adaptable and efficient and facilitating freedom to test what you're building on the edges

Together, they facilitate active strategy: planning, taking action, evaluating results, and circling back to inform the next move. By making space for this active learning process, my marketing strategies are more useful for my clients, and they achieve better results.

A word of caution: it's easy to get swept up in real-time analytics from Google, Instagram, and Facebook ads. Surrounded by the grow-fast-or-die business culture, it can be tempting to use those figures to chase short-term results. But it's important to question and determine how that strategy aligns with your goals. A business that wants to sell in two years, for example, operates very differently than a business that wants to endure for twenty years. It's a different game, with different goals. Either goal is fine, but they require different strategies to accomplish.

This is where your traditional documentation can keep you grounded and anchored to the true core of your endeavor. And it's also why taking the time to dig deep to be able to name your core intention (e.g., your Epic Center and Epic Outcome) is so important. Remember, our goal isn't merely to generate growth but to create a Groundswell. The magnitude of this impact requires you to think differently—to change your attention span from fast growth to ongoing, sustainable growth.

REJECTING PATIENCE

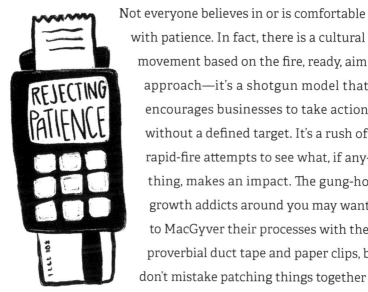

Not everyone believes in or is comfortable with patience. In fact, there is a cultural movement based on the fire, ready, aim approach—it's a shotgun model that encourages businesses to take action without a defined target. It's a rush of rapid-fire attempts to see what, if anything, makes an impact. The gung-ho growth addicts around you may want to MacGyver their processes with the proverbial duct tape and paper clips, but don't mistake patching things together for being resourceful—they are not the same.

There was a time when I bought into all of that "10x, get-rich-fast-ask-questions-later" mentality. Unfortunately, this mindset usually emanates from a place of scarcity. Now I recognize that approach is not a strategy; it's fear of missing out, and fear will get you and your Groundswell nowhere.

Not only that, but charging ahead without gathering the necessary pieces into place is potentially dangerous. Rushing growth—perhaps breezing through the Build phase or skipping it altogether—comes at a high cost to your Groundswell. Resources like time, money, and energy are finite, and when you don't take the time to think ahead, you risk wasting them. The cost is not just financial; it also comes at the price of other intangible essentials like morale and momentum.

Remember, though, that patience is not twiddling your thumbs waiting for your audience to find you. It's mindfully taking the right action and allowing time to see the results. It's not waiting to get started—it's having the courage to stay the course. It's trusting yourself and your vision, and then doing the work to make it come to life.

HIT THE BUTTON

A few years ago, I worked for one of Canada's oldest and largest national retailers. We identified that they were spending significant amounts of their annual marketing budget on full-page magazine ads that featured their business-to-business gift cards. The problem was that there was no method of measurement attached to demonstrate the effectiveness and impact of the campaign. In large part, the company ran the ads because it was a fast and simple way to market, as though doing something was better than nothing, even though they had no idea whether what they did was even effective. It was simply an action for action's sake.

Sometimes you need to hit Reset.

We challenged our client to first add the ability to track traffic and source any new leads that may have come from the magazine campaign. Over a very short period of time, it became clear that these ads were not only ineffective but also extremely expensive. Talk about economic waste. It was our strategy to then redistribute those funds into different programs and campaigns that would (1) be measurable, and (2) build relationships. Our theory was that these less expensive, ongoing efforts would be much more sustainable and effective.

ADD VALUE VERSUS ADS

Our solution was to directly mail personalized gift cards to the company's high-value clients to directly demonstrate the service and experience their customers could expect when buying from them. In essence: showing, not telling. Granted, the campaign took more time to plan and build all the components, but the results were undeniable. It performed so well that the program went on for many years, and over time the cost of marketing went down significantly. Those leftover funds went into developing and testing new marketing ideas and programs, allowing us the resources to experiment and innovate.

Most of the time, a highly intentional and personalized approach to marketing—one that adds value, not just running an ad—is going to get the results you're after. Poorly designed and executed strategies can only create short-term impressions that seek to simply convince your audience to purchase. This is a wind swell—a quick result that dies down soon after it begins, and a far less powerful wave than a Groundswell. Sure, sometimes you get lucky. But you can't build sustainability on luck.

Instead, Groundswelling begins with ample and adequate time in the Build phase, where you pour your energy and ideas into your strategy, frontloading it with potential. Give yourself permission to think deeper, bigger, and longer about what matters most to your audience—what value are you offering for their time, attention, and action? How can you communicate that value clearly?

PATIENCE VERSUS QUITTING

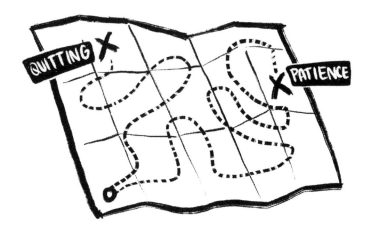

"I never lose. I either win or learn."

—Nelson Mandela

Whenever we begin something, it's equally important to talk about quitting. In their book *Rework*, Jason Fried and David Heinemeier Hansson wrote, "People automatically associate quitting with failure, but sometimes that's exactly what you should do. If you already spent too much time on something that wasn't worth it, walk away. You can't get that time back. The worst thing you can do now is waste even more time."

This is not to say you should throw in your towel at the first sign of trouble. Don't amputate your leg because of a stubbed toe! It's simply acknowledging that quitting isn't the antithesis to patience. The difference is knowing whether you're moving in your desired direction. When that's clear, you feel empowered to move forward, either by pressing through or calling it quits.

If you find your plan is not working, and you're not achieving the results you want, look closer.

- Have you shared your vision, values, and value proposition with the wrong audience?
- Or is it the right audience, but you're sharing a wrong/unclear message, making it impossible to communicate to your ideal audience?

Neither of these are instant deal breakers. It just means there's more Building to do. A good start is to check back in with the Origins of your Groundswell.

- What is your macro vision—your Epic Center and Epic Outcome?
- What are your micro goals? What specifically are you trying to do right now?
- Who are the best people to help you accomplish these micro goals? Why should they care?
- What are the best message and best method to communicate your vision to this specific audience? How will

people know that your vision does (or does not) apply to them?

- What's the immediate impact? How can you give people what they want and make them want to be part of what you are doing?
- And finally, an essential but often overlooked aspect of any strategic plan: what are you going to measure to ensure you're on the right track? How are you going to measure it?

All that said, many well-meaning entrepreneurs are going after growth when their industry is sunsetting or the environment is shifting. Don't be the guy who tried to build a fax machine when the world just started onboarding email. If you find yourself trying to build in an outdated and irrelevant industry, quit and quit early. No amount of long-suffering and patience is going to get you what you want. Your time is valuable, so spend it on things that are worthy of your energy. Otherwise, eventually you will quit or be out of business, wondering what went wrong. Cut your losses and make room for something better.

On the flipside, when you have clarity in your mission, and it's congruent with your values, always be innovating. Sometimes, quitting is precisely the pivot you need. It doesn't mean you failed; it means each obstacle taught you a better way forward. This is what patient, active strategy looks like.

A Groundswell Parable:
A Vision Worth Shaping

Patience is a virtue because it's not always easy. When building a business, we may be tempted to rush ahead to "make
something happen," but patience is a practice—something
we choose to intentionally cultivate every day, especially
when we're anxious to see results.

This level of intention is the first lesson Koa and Kalani had
to learn.

Koa was eager to get out of his retail job and devote all his
time to making custom boards. To do so, they needed to
increase sales enough to offset the loss of income he would

incur, as well as have enough to cover costs of increased materials and overhead. To make this happen, Kalani learned how to run ads and target middle-aged surfing enthusiasts who were fascinated by Koa's techniques.

It worked! They gained lots of attention and sales, so much that not only could Koa quit his retail job—he *had* to quit to keep up with demand. Koa worked around the clock for two months straight fulfilling all the orders. This surge in growth came at a cost—because Koa wanted to specialize in custom boards, he offered a wide variety of materials to choose from. That meant that he kept a lot of different materials on hand, each coming from a different supplier. Additionally, because he allowed every buyer to choose their specific material, it was difficult to prep and have boards roughed out in general shape, waiting to be customized based on specifications. This meant Koa was always starting from scratch, which put him behind.

The perceived benefit of offering his buyers choice wasn't serving the business or, it turns out, those he was creating for.

Kalani encouraged Koa to streamline his process by limiting the options he offered his customers. This felt like a step backward to Koa, like he was shrinking his business. It wasn't until the siblings watched a documentary about ocean plastic that Koa saw an authentic path forward. Together, they decided to pivot their model to a surf shop that specialized in custom boards made from recycled ocean plastic.

This was a niche market compared to what they had been targeting before. But it allowed Koa to narrow the scope of materials and focus more on his designs and techniques. Their business embraced their identity as boutique rather than trying to compete with mass market. Instead of a race to the bottom in terms of quality and price, they recognized the value of crafting small batches of high-quality boards at a higher price point.

When you have clarity in your mission and it's congruent with your values, keep adjusting and innovating to find the way forward. Align yourself firmly to that vision and hold every decision you make to that standard. Ask yourself, "Is this direction and action authentically aligned with my Epic End?" Then learn from each mistake or obstacle that pops up along the way. This is what being patient with your plan looks like.

A NOTE
ABOUT AUTHENTICITY

*"You only have control over three things in your life—
the thoughts you think, the images you visualize, and
the actions you take."*

—Jack Canfield

To build a Groundswell, your vision, focus, and actions need to be congruent from the very start. Not only that, but they must be original and authentic to you. In their book *Authenticity*, Joe Pine and James Gilmore write that there are two key principles to consider on the subject: (1) being true to your own self, and (2) being who you say you are to others. As they put it:

> Authenticity, we believe, flows from these two principles of thought and action. Together, they help us ascertain the real in an otherwise amorphous landscape. First, the importance of being earnest, consistent, and self-directed centers one on one's perception of oneself. Second, being trustworthy, honest, and compassionate focuses one on one's behavior towards others.

During the Build phase is when you have the most control and ability to invest in your thoughts and actions. Attempts that are shallow, fake, or inauthentic won't connect deeply enough to make a lasting impact. You can and should take the time to really sink into and name your origins—your thoughts, ideas, inspirations for original product designs or innovations on existing industry, the specific audience you want to serve, and the impact you want to create. These are the foundation from which you authentically Build.

Later in *Authenticity*, Joe Pine and James Gilmore emphasize the importance of origin and history:

Consider: *Where* and *when* you came to be who you are today—the place and time in which the enterprise and its offerings originated—with the subsequent history of each in the world, generating the story of who you are today. Companies, as with people, are the products of nature and nurturing. The circumstances of their inception foundationally shape their identity.

If you're new, create your heritage. If you have a history, bring it to life. Either way, you have to live up to the attributes of this declared heritage.

Own your authenticity and your role as the source and storm of your Groundswell. The force of your clarity becomes your brand and reputation. Not only does this propel you forward, but it also creates a barrier to the competition. Those who would try to replicate you are found to be shallow. As they say, "There can only be one original."

Ultimately, when you embrace the fullness of your vision, without apology, you tap the wave of hidden potential like nothing else can.

THE UNCOMMON BUILD

"NEW SCHOOL THINKING OLD SCHOOL COMMON SENSE"

When viewed in the context of how a Groundswell is generated, the Build phase begins with the storm of origin, when the initial energy of inspiration breaks through the surface, sending waves of possibility in every direction. This seems like new-school thinking, but it isn't. In the Build phase, you mindfully align those frenetic waves, combining and uniting them, and sending them in the direction of the shore where you desire to make your Epic Outcome.

It just makes common sense to take the time to Build.

Another useful way to think of the Build is as pulling back the string of a bow for the arrow. Feel yourself creating tension in the opposite direction you are going. In the moment, it might feel counterintuitive, but when you reach the height of that tension and release, the arrow soars forward with the power and momentum to reach your target.

The key to unlocking the Build phase of your Groundswell is patient action and strategic hustle. Anyone can take action, but not everyone can be mindful and patient in the actions they take. Patient strategy produces bold action that captures momentum, and this leads to results.

Patience is not passive; it's mindfully active: a determined, focused, and tenacious pursuit. One that strategically scouts for opportunities to sprint and grow quickly, all the while building and gaining bit by bit by bit. As you move incrementally in the right direction, you learn to accelerate your energy in that direction toward what's working. Even setbacks highlight the next right step. Through this lens, failure, too, is forward progress. Remember, when your goal is a Groundswell, you aren't competing against others—only yourself. Regardless of how you compare to a competitor, if you're making an impact, you are succeeding.

The principles of patience, mindfulness, and strategy are not solely confined to the Build phase. Like a Groundswell itself, once an element is put into motion, it keeps going, carrying forward into everything that comes after.

CONNECTION IS THE NEW CASH

"Before people can buy from you,
they've got to buy into you."

—Chuck D, Public Enemy

Today's growth-obsessed culture expects a business to push their product or service straight out of the gates. To design something and then saturate the market with promotion for it, regardless of whether it is useful or ideal for the client. It's about the sale and the sale alone.

When people—in the form of followers, subscribers, or visitors—enter your marketing ecosystem, the impulse is often to look for the immediate return. If your funnel is unable to convert them to a sale of some kind, you presume failure and the people as nothing more than dead weight. This perspective is all too common and misses the entire point of building an audience, because it only views connection in terms of transactions.

To build something that lasts, we must see our audience as humans first. Not customers, not consumers, not targets…humans.

HUMANS NOT CUSTOMER$

HUMANS,
NOT CUSTOMERS

Business and marketing come down to a remarkably simple principle: humans want to be valued and receive value. When your business offers something that is meaningful—that is, when you provide a way for the audience to find meaning in it themselves—it meets this need to be connected to deeper meaning and generates value that becomes like connective tissue to everything you do, connecting your audience to you. But that's not what happens when we chase transactions; there is less meaningful connection.

Transactions are quick, single-serve experiences that generally lack meaning; but when you take the time to value your audience as humans first, you build long-term investments in the form of relationships—which will always outweigh transactions, no matter what today's sales numbers say. Relationships create the opportunity for more than just a short-term transaction. They plant seeds of loyalty, which can grow to numerous, recurring transactions in the future. But if you only seek the one-time quick transaction now, that's all you'll have.

To shift this focus, instead of looking at your audience as a target to hit, recognize that they are valued friends whose lives you can enrich.

In his book *To Sell Is Human*, Daniel H. Pink shines a light on a surprising truth: when your methods for connecting to your audience are genuine and for the highest good, the value of your interactions increases and consequently results in transactions. He calls this up*serving*, a contrast to up*selling*.

Upserving means doing more for the other person than they expect or than you initially intended, taking those extra steps that transform a mundane interaction into a memorable experience. This simple shift from upselling to upserving has the obvious advantage of being the right thing to do, but it's also extraordinarily effective.

Rather than, "How can I sell this immediately?" ask, "How can we serve our audience better?"

Rather than, "How can we motivate a transaction?" ask, "How can we help them individually?"

The results of this shift in perspective? Imagine the difference from a hundred sales today to a thousand views tomorrow to three thousand true fans for years to come.

That said, creating genuine relationships with your audience is not easy, and most businesses grossly underestimate the process. With the sheer volume of marketing messages that your audience sees on a daily basis, the majority of which are shallow and transaction-focused, their attention span collapses. They check out to survive.

Big marketing pushes may gain their attention momentarily, and may even result in a sale, but this amounts to nothing more than a symptom of short-termism. The attention won't last. As Seth Godin says in his book *Tribes*, "The opportunity is not in being momentarily popular with the anonymous masses. It's in being missed when you're gone, in doing work that matters to the tribe you choose."

Building an audience requires more than big marketing that garners attention. Focusing on mindful connection will enable you to supersede attention and achieve captivation. And it is building this *captive audience* that creates the solid foundation to generate your Groundswell and grow your business.

BUILD YOUR AUDIENCE BEFORE YOU NEED IT

Building relationships is a direct result of patience, mindfulness, and strategy; but that doesn't mean you have to wait to begin creating high-quality connections. As the ancient proverb says, "Dig a well before you're thirsty." In Groundswelling, this applies to your audience.

And while the methods of marketing have changed dramatically over the last three decades, people haven't. Building an audience is about focusing on what matters most to them: their needs. A business, and certainly a Groundswell, is founded on meeting people's needs. Despite our unique differences and circumstances, as humans we all have the same foundational needs. Tony Robbins describes them as certainty, uncertainty/variety, significance, love/connection, growth, and contribution. We'll discuss these in more detail in future sections, but for now, we carry forward the concept of focusing on what our audience needs, not just what we want them to buy.

As Seth Godin says in *Tribes*, "Don't find customers for your products. Find products for your customers." This means you need to have an audience first. Instead of creating goods and services and then hiring marketing consultants to find you customers, reverse it. Build an audience you want to serve and learn from them. Build trust and earn their buy-in. Then create goods and services that meet their needs and share your offerings with them.

This is not just a feel-good way to serve others; it is also extremely practical. Building an audience first allows you to (1) gain rapid feedback, and (2) build interest for future offerings.

When you gather your audience in advance, you can vet your ideas before committing to something expensive and unproven. The audience-first strategy taps the "planning paradox" mentioned in the Patience chapter by allowing you to take some action now in order to gain feedback. This provides you the opportunity to make adjustments and get it right, so you can maximize connection in your future actions.

Not everyone who connects with you will be a customer, but even those who aren't might be supporters—and that's important, too. Advocates, allies, and influencers all have a part to play when building a Groundswell. Members of a community are connected beyond commerce. They create a cooperative connection around a common interest. Seth Godin explains it like this:

A tribe is a group of people connected to one another, connected to a leader, and connected to an idea. For millions of years, human beings have been part of one tribe or another. A group needs only two things to be a tribe: a shared interest and a way to communicate.

When you cultivate an audience around a similar need, passion, or interest, you can Build from there and identify deeper, more specific needs—which allows you to craft goods and services that truly serve your audience. It may take longer, but the payoff is of Groundswell proportions.

You can strategize the path to your ideal audience using the Blueprint.

IDEATE | DIFFERENTIATE | ACTIVATE

Ideate

You need to imagine the audience that could carry the scope of your vision. How big does your reach need to be to hit the shore of Epic Outcome?

When you apply our thinking to building an audience, you want to first identify an audience you want to serve. We create relationships by meeting one another's needs, either through fulfilling a specific need or providing connection around a shared one. To do this well with your clients and customers, you must first understand their needs. Clothing, food, entertainment, and empathy all meet needs. There's no point in trying to do everything. Instead, focus on being aware and mindful of customers' needs and finding the way to best serve them and make the most impact.

It's also important that you can identify your ideal audience in the wild. Where do they hang out? Think about the various events, platforms, and channels. Forum websites like Reddit are full of niche markets with unmet needs. By joining the conversation, you can learn what matters to potential customers and provide value by answering questions in your specific area of expertise and influence. This can be part of your active strategy to go where your tribe gathers, listen, and then engage.

Bottom line: find where your audience is and listen, so you can identify their needs well.

Differentiate

Everyone is unique in where they gather information and how they communicate for different transactions and activities. For example, businesspeople may prefer to talk business on LinkedIn or by phone, and use text and Instagram for their social connections. So, consider how people connect (the medium), in what form (the content), and how they process the content (the learning that takes place).

Just before Christmas of 2020, my understanding of these dynamics increased by leaps and bounds. I started to spend some time on the app Clubhouse, which is an audio-only mobile app where you can connect with other people and discuss various topics in chat rooms. I wanted to test the idea of "Mindful Marketing," so I set up a room every Sunday and brought in some top experts on the panel. I started the first room with only five people and my co-host, Victoria; three months later, we had a fanatical following where rooms consistently lasted for three or four hours with hundreds of people. I would get messages from people about how "they found their tribe." This was such a unique room, they felt at home, and we absolutely felt like we had hit a nerve of connection with hundreds of people. We were told that it became one of the most sought-after rooms on Clubhouse during that time.

When connecting with your ideal audience, if you differentiate how you communicate and engage, you can unlock so much insight into how to engage customers on a human level.

Activate

When it comes to your audience, you may create multiple communities around the same good because different segments of your audience connect with it in different ways. The way you meet the needs of each community will be different, too. For example, the soap company Dove might build a community around skincare and a community around self-image. The skincare audience would be interested in practical use, while the self-image audience would be engaged by a conversation about the internal definitions of beauty. The content curated or created to serve these audiences would be unique.

Whatever your levels of activity are in the moment, the mindset should be that you're in this to help and to build the relationship. This is vastly different from the traditional transactional mindset, in which no relationship is cultivated between buyer and seller. The relationship mindset begins with a totally different intention, energy, and investment for the long-term.

Bottom line, activate your audience by directly connecting on a one-on-one basis. To do this well, you can't stay on the surface. For a Groundswell-worthy connection, you need to go subterranean.

A DEEPER LEVEL OF CONNECTION

To connect with someone, you've got to get on their level. The most effective kind of connection happens when an audience's core values are directly aligned with the brand's core values. And it's more than just seeing eye-to-eye; we're talking about soul-to-soul connection.

When we say deep, think subterranean-deep.

This deeper level of connection requires commitment to the journey of understanding your audience's deeper needs. This may be something they can't even name yet, but it's there, going unmet.

In the end, a good or service is really just a representation of core values. Connecting and serving at the core level means connecting with your audience—not just around what they want, but with the foundational *values* they hold. The deeper unmet need is for more of these foundational values to be present in their life.

A connection to values creates a new way to identify who you want to serve. Replace traditional demographics with *value*graphics. This shift in thinking is a fundamental disruption to predict what people will do next based on what people value, because what we value determines what we do. It does not rely on guesswork, opinion, and broad assumptions about how people act based on age or other vague identifiers.

The tricky part is that everyone measures values differently. One person's garbage is another person's treasure. While there are many things that humans universally value, the hierarchy of importance we place on them will differ from group to group and individual to individual. These differences can be very nuanced.

CONNECTING ON VALUES CREATES BUY-IN

David Allison, founder of Valuegraphics, says "What we value determines what we do, so the people who love your brand will have shared values." Allison collected more than half a million surveys in 152 languages from around the world, asking people what they value, want, need, and expect in life. The result is the first-ever purpose-built dataset of contextualized values that scientifically demonstrates this approach, which can be accessed through his company. Despite our previous faith in demographics to find our ideal audience, the most effective audience for you to name is not going to be uniform in age, race, or gender—it will be people who have the same values as you.

The consulting firm Bain & Company created a pyramid of values broken into different tiers: functional values, emotional values, and aspirational values.[7]

---

[7]   Eric Almquist, John Senior, and Nicolas Bloch, "The Elements of Value," *Harvard Business Review*, August 8, 2016, https://www.bain.com/insights/the-elements-of-value-hbr/.

- Functional values may be things such as "save time" or "save money." They are commoditized or a basic requirement for some level of differentiation.
- Emotional values create a deeper connection with feelings—e.g., "fun and entertaining"—or have design aesthetics appeal.
- Aspirational values are about self-actualization, hope, and self-transcendence. They are about going into a deeper sense of purpose.

This value structure aligns with Maslow's famous hierarchy of needs, but it also goes further to break down the various values and needs that exist within each level.

We've all gotten used to giving up what we value most because few companies offer us their product in the way we would value it the most. Instead, we have to accept the best we can find. Recognizing this niche value is an opportunity. Whether someone prioritizes convenience over quality or variety over consistency, people will pay for what they value as long they can see it. If you can name the core values of your business, you can find the people who share those values. But an audience won't connect with you unless your values are broadcast loud and clear.

This is where people buy *into* you versus just buying *from* you.

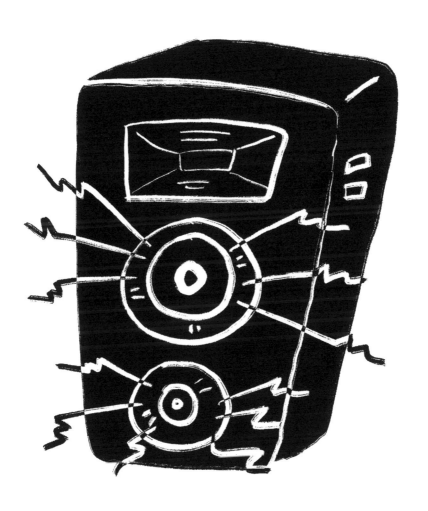

COMMUNICATING VALUE

When your values are communicated well, your audience sees more than a product they want—they recognize you as part of their tribe and one of their own.

This uniting based on core values is an essential component of Groundswelling. There are specific methods you can use to communicate your values and connect with your audience.

In *The Long and Short of It*, Peter Field and Les Binet highlight a distinction between rational messaging/activation and emotional priming. These two approaches serve different functions when it comes to generating short-term and long-term growth. Think of it as addressing both sides of your brain—what moves you and what you logically think you should be doing. The combination appeals to both sides of your brain, and you are therefore more likely to take action.

Rational Messaging as Activation

Rational messages are about logic and taking action now. Remember the "elements of value"? This rational messaging is very much tied to functional value—basic information that adds up and that you can logically move forward with. Example: *Buy now! Fifteen percent off! Only ten left!* This is rational messaging—looking at the savings and the importance of making the decision to purchase now.

The downside to these kinds of messages is that they are often quickly forgotten. After the moment of purchase, members of the target audience cease to pay close attention, and the results quickly decay. With few residual effects on brand perceptions, long-term sales, or price elasticity, the long-term paybacks are modest.

Rational messaging works great at the time of purchase but doesn't do enough to inspire a groundswell of support for future interaction and purchases. If your competitors present a more rational message, you can potentially lose your connection with your audience.

Luckily, we have another kind of messaging to help with that.

Emotional Messaging as Priming

Emotional messages are intended to (you guessed it) move you emotionally and pull at your heartstrings. Example: *Wouldn't your loved one appreciate you buying this for them?* This can happen through words, music, sound, smell…any stimulus that primes the desired emotional connection for your brand, message, or interaction. Emotional messaging requires far less attention and active interest in the moment because it's stimulating our senses at a primal level. The more senses engaged, the more profound the emotions, and therefore the more primed a person will be to connect to the feeling, message, and desired action.

But because of this primal aspect of feelings, the effect of the feeling stays with them long after they've forgotten the content of the message. The message's impact lingers. Emotional priming communicates not only to imminent purchasers, but future and potential ones, too. Repeated exposures can lead to even more deepened emotional connection, furthering this effect. The result of this long-lasting emotional impact is long-term sales growth, and an audience willing to pay more because they see a deeper value.

Imagine what's possible when we combine the power of activation and priming into one message.

DO BOTH

SALES ACTIVATION
—SHORT-TERM SALES UPLIFT—

BRAND BUILDING
—LONG-TERM SALES GROWTH—

SALES UPLIFT OVER BASE

TIME

SHORT-TERM EFFECTS DOMINATE

Connect to One Wavelength

Over my many years of working with clients on their brand strategy and messaging, one of the keys to provoking responses from their audiences is to blend rational messaging with some emotional messaging. Leveraging the hidden forces of both emotions and rationality can generate the optimal wave of connection—one that is powerful, compelling, and captivating for your audience.

This chart demonstrates how, and why, rational messaging tends to dominate short-term effects, while emotional priming dominates long-term effects. As Field and Binet explain: "Emotional priming makes people more receptive to rational messages, and so amplifies short-term responses. Rational activation unlocks the short-term sales potential of the brand, converting brand equity more powerfully into sales." If you can understand this distinction and then, ideally, execute a "multi-channel campaign…designed to provoke both kinds of response in balance…effects are optimized over all timescales."

In essence, you are leaving impact on the table by focusing on just one approach—emotional or rational—and therefore only impacting one aspect: short-term or long-term. This is a mouthful, so you may need to read it twice:

- Emotional priming makes people more receptive to rational messages, and so amplifies short-term responses.
- Rational activation unlocks the short-term sales potential of the brand, converting brand equity more powerfully into sales.

Woven together, each adds value to the other, strengthening the impact of the message. With blending, you can have it all. Yes, *have it all!* Mixing sales activation with brand-building activities makes you effective and efficient, now and in the future.

As Field and Binet note, "Although most kinds of marketing communications provoke both [rational and emotional] response to a degree, the balance varies widely." My observation is that even marketers who use both still focus too much on one type or the other. A full-spectrum messaging cocktail—one that is emotionally compelling and makes rational sense—is a powerful way to get people to buy in. In that case, again, the ideal scenario is "multi-channel campaigns…designed to provoke both kinds of response in balance, [ensuring] that effects are optimized over all timescales." So, mix that cocktail!

The One Wavelength

When you do find that mix, you create a single, stronger wavelength that keeps you in balance and creates an ecosystem of sustainable desire and response to build your Groundswell. Turns out, the only rational response to an emotional connection of deeply shared values is a commitment. And I have found no bigger impact than connecting with people's *values*.

When I built my following on Clubhouse, I intentionally used the term Mindful Marketing to signal to my potential audience what I valued. The term Mindful Marketing is a fun juxtaposition; it pairs the slow, methodical, and present state of mindfulness with the passionate, extroverted determination of marketing. Rather than tapping the functional value of "how to market to make money," or even the emotional value of "how to market without feeling icky," we took it a step further and layered in aspirational value: "Be a mindful marketer who is effective yet connects to your deeper purpose and magnetizes people to you."

This is where the juice is.

Tapping aspirational values can generate a completely irrational response, one that is not sensitive to price and is willing to overlook logic because it connects with something more meaningful than money. But aspirational values alone are not sustainable—anchor them with functional and emotional values.

This layered approach to messaging wages war against the tyranny of short-term thinking and unlocks even more of your hidden marketing potential. Connection becomes your currency when you start with these steps:

1. Name your core values (as seen through the lens of your Epic Center and Epic Outcome).
2. Identify the ideal audience who shares those deeply held values.
3. Craft and deliver a message that speaks to both the rational and emotional elements of those values, thereby activating a stronger wavelength that becomes the siren song your audience will find irresistible.

TAP INTO THE EXPERIENCE ECONOMY

*"People will forget what you said, people will
forget what you did, but people will never
forget how you made them feel."*

—Maya Angelou

Building a Groundswell is about impacting and
improving people's lives. It requires crossing
the chasm from having a customer to being
in community and fostering an ongoing
client relationship. This progression
requires a clear understanding of the
customer experience.

Today's consumers are tired of
being walking billboards and
are less likely than ever to wear
branded goods. For many people, it feels like being put in a
box rather than representing
their unique, individual selves.
Instead of blindly buying
brands, consumers are purchas-
ing goods that align with who they are and what they want to
stand for.

—

This has always been the case to some degree, but the abundance of choices and customization available in today's market has shifted it to a whole new level—from a nice-to-have to a must-have. The ability to be true to themselves through their purchases creates a demand for the personalization of goods, services, and experiences through community and connection in their transactions. Niche is now the standard.

So, in a market of personalization, how do you stand out?

By staging a stellar experience.

Your audience's desire for a personal experience is critical to the way you design your customer journey. You want to create an experience that is memorable and potentially transformational. When we tap deeper into human needs, offering more than just a good or service, we connect with the experience we aim for our audience to have. It will exceed their expectations. Experiences allow you to meet your audience's needs on a more personal level and deliver deeper and more meaningful connection.

When it comes to understanding where customer behavior will be in the future, author Joe Pine is a sought-after business advisor. He's identified some of the biggest structural shifts in economic offerings that are impacting business today. In his book *The Experience Economy*, written with James Gilmore, Pine identified industry shifts in business thinking around how to create experiences as an economic offering. This has since transformed the market as we know it, making it more customized and personal than ever before.

Joe Pine holds a vision that, in the future, we won't refer to the process of disseminating our messages related to goods and services as *marketing*. Instead, we'll call it customering (coined by James Gilmore). It will no longer be about capturing the market, but about aligning with the variety of unique needs in each individual. The idea of customering is to honor the individual experience with more deeply personalized human connection, from mass market to target market to niche market to one-to-one marketing, and all the way to multiple markets within a single individual.

When I reviewed this portion of the book with Joe Pine, he articulated that every customer wants different things at different times with different offerings. You are not the same individual in every circumstance. Something to really think about is how to connect with the uniqueness of the individual in each moment and in every interaction.

LEARNING TO CONNECT

Learning how to better serve your audience never stops. In fact, it should only accelerate once you convert an audience member into a customer. Joe Pine, Martha Rogers, and Don Peppers came up with a framework called "learning relationships," which they explain in their industry-changing article in the *Harvard Business Review* entitled "Do You Want to Keep Your Customers Forever?"[8] They show us that a learning relationship is an ongoing connection between a business and a consumer that becomes smarter as the two interact with each other, collaborating to meet the consumer's needs over time.

---

[8] B. Joseph Pine II, Don Peppers, and Martha Rogers, "Do You Want to Keep Your Customers Forever?" *Harvard Business Review*, March–April 1995, https://hbr.org/1995/03/do-you-want-to-keep-your-customers-forever.

In learning relationships, individual customers teach the company more and more about their preferences and needs, giving the company an immense competitive advantage. The more customers teach the company, the better it becomes at providing exactly what they want—exactly how they want it—and the more difficult it will be for a competitor to entice them away. Even if a competitor were to build the exact same capabilities, a customer already involved in a learning relationship with a company would have to spend an inordinate amount of time and energy teaching the competitor what the company already knows.

What if in the Build phase you took the time to bake into your systems ways to learn and capture this information so you could lock in your audience's imagination, support, and commitment forever? Don Peppers has this to say:

> What I tell companies is, if you think treating customers right and delivering a really good experience to them is costly, the only reason you think that is because you're working on the wrong timeframe. The truth is it's the most fruitful kind of investment you could possibly make. The returns are in the future, not this quarter. It might cost you money today, but it's going to return many more times than that tomorrow.[9]

---

[9] Scott A. Martin, "Don Peppers | Trust Is the New Currency," January 6, 2020, in *Groundswell Origins*, podcast, 1:03:00, https://groundswellorigins.com/podcast/don-peppers-2.

Stage experiences to make your Groundswell surge, build, and grow. Soon you will be moving into the next phase, creating change and ultimately guiding your audience into the wave of Transformation.

A Groundswell Parable:
Search for a Direct Connection

Koa and Kalani have always had one very important thing going for them—they are great at making connections.

In his town, Koa is known as the go-to guy for all things surf—where to surf, when to surf. His workshop is open to the public, and he is happy to talk surf all day with anyone who stops by. Kalani started making videos of Koa in the shop and on the beach, sharing Koa's tips and insights about surfing and conservation with their growing online community.

Always on the lookout for their next growth opportunity, Koa and Kalani attend a surf convention and make a powerful impression on a California retail chain that becomes interested in stocking Groundswell Goods surfboards in their stores. With a contract guaranteeing inventory sales for the next twelve months, to be sold in surf shops up and down the California coast, this is an amazing opportunity to increase Groundswell Goods' exposure and bottom line. The certainty factor makes Koa eager to accept the offer.

But Kalani is more cautious. The contract would require an increase in production, upping Koa's work quota and forcing him to work at a more rapid pace. Even if they brought on an apprentice, it's unlikely they would also be able to keep their Etsy shop going, as all their time and effort would need to go toward fulfilling the retail contract. On top of that, this pace would not allow Koa the flow he currently enjoys and the interactions he has with his local surf community. Business might be booming on the inside, but the indirect model would create a scarcity of their number one resource: Koa's knowledge, expertise, and presence.

Kalani chooses to look at the problem differently: how could they better leverage Koa's powerful presence and interactions with fellow surf enthusiasts? Rather than sign a contract to distribute with another business, Kalani suggests they open their own customer-facing retail shop. This way, they can maintain their online direct-to-customer relationships through their Etsy store, as well as establish a storefront for their own direct-to-customer interactions. And best of all, Koa could continue at his pace and flow and engage with the community in a way that feels natural.

When it comes to connection, strategy is part of the equation. For Groundswell Goods, the key to connection was to shift their mindset from searching for transactions to increasing the quality of their relationships. They turn down the chance to do more business indirectly and instead choose to focus on direct interactions with the surfers they want to serve, and further shape the experience of their audience.

PLAYING THE LONG GAME

I love this quote by Seth Godin, from *This is Marketing*.

> There's a groundswell of people doing marketing because they can
> make things better. They're prepared to engage with the market
> because they know they can contribute to our culture. People like
> you.

When you're building a long game, the metrics start with attention.
Then come followers, subscribers, and—finally—customers. The
entire process has hidden potential to accelerate your growth,
but it takes time.

World-renowned entrepreneur Gary Vaynerchuk has a long-term vision to own the New York Jets. But this goal began with his long-term mindset, and he is using it to build an audience and gain their attention. This is simply step one of his bigger vision. He builds connection by publicly sharing this plan—including breaking down his steps of cash and connection to the various audiences he needs, from divisions of athlete representation to Super Bowl marketing. He is building an audience by connecting with the community to support his grand vision, *and* selling to this audience. Even if he never reaches his long-term goal, he has built a Groundswell of attention and growth for all his business interests along the way.

I have spent the last eight years preparing for this book and launching the *Groundswell Marketing Podcast*. Right now, I have thousands of followers across social networks, and people are starting to notice. It has taken me years of posting content and engaging daily.

When you know where your long game is headed, you can feel confident in the process—as long as there is movement. Movement is key to growth. When you plant a seed, nothing is visible on the surface, but just because you can't see it doesn't mean it's not growing. Keep planting and watering your seeds. The long game knows that sustainable growth is not realized by getting caught up in the size of your audience, but instead by focusing on engagement and relationship.

As you produce interesting content and provide value, you will build an audience. But beware: many marketers get caught up in building an audience without actually building a client base. A large portion of the audience can grow into passive observers rather than connected members. As every master gardener knows, it takes a great deal of planning, patience, planting, watering, and weeding to cultivate a beautiful garden. But they also know you can't single-handedly be the source of a garden's vitality; and, at some point, you've got to stop watering dead plants. It can be hard to accept this, especially when you've worked so hard to grow what you have.

But if growth is the goal, you have to adapt when something's no longer life-giving. It's the same with your customer base. Let's say you have ten thousand followers but barely five hundred are active customers. Don't waste vital time, resources, and energy on the 9,500 who aren't engaged. Devote that time to cultivating customers who are yielding vital growth. Sure, you can keep pouring into unresponsive aspects of your audience, hoping they will come to life. But sometimes you just have to move on and remove the dead weight to make room for new seedlings to grow.

THE BUILDING BLOCKS TO
A DEEPER LAYER OF CONNECTION

To generate a Groundswell, you must first build connection with a core, loyal audience. This bond is built not through transactions, but through a community of shared value. When you seek out this audience early, before you're selling anything, you have the potential to create true fans who align with your vision and carry your message forward.

To mindfully serve humans, rather than simply acquire customers, remember not to confuse attention with connection. You may win a stranger's attention by yelling at them from across the street; but without nurturing and cultivating trust, even in that simple moment, their attention will fizzle and result in nothing more than a turn of their head, when what you want is for them to cross to you and shake your hand so you can buy them lunch.

Think of connection + trust = action. Start your connection with an intention of building trust versus attention, and the audience reaction will be a deeper layer of connection to you and your brand.

UPSERVE: THE NEW UPSELL

Once you make that initial connection, don't focus on upsell, but shift into upserve. Not only will you feel more human and the people you serve feel more connected, but you will be actively building the foundation you need. These relationships will be the armature—a spine of strength—upon which you can build even more. In other words, the transactions will come.

Connection is not an event, but a process. As you move forward with an intention to connect with your ideal audience, do so in the most meaningful and intimate way you can based on your current resources and reality. When you seek to serve people rather than sell to them, you tap into your unique path of connection—one that is unstoppable.

"A brand is simply trust."

—Steve Jobs

We are leaving the age of attention and entering the age of trust. Attention is fleeting; trust is hard to come by. Relationships are the cornerstone of a Groundswell, but this applies to more than your audience. To truly leverage the power of relationship, you must build connections not just with your audience, but across every aspect of your business. In other words, you must build a brand. Since you're pursuing a Groundswell, no doubt you understand that your brand is not simply your logo, color palette, or web design. It's not even the goods and services you offer. In fact, your brand is not what *you* say at all.

Your brand is the way *others* perceive you.

And while the first impression of your appearance does matter, it is a fragment of your brand. Think of an individual person: while they may be perceived a certain way based on their appearance, it's their actions that teach the world who they really are. Your brand is the culmination of the impressions your business leaves on others.

Just as a rancher wields a literal brand that leaves a permanent mark on the animals in their care, your interactions with others will also leave an impression of how you made them feel. The stronger the feeling, the more likely they are to share their experience with others. Word of mouth is the force that solidifies and amplifies a brand, for better or worse.

How do you ensure it is for the better?

Author and branding consultant Wally Olins puts it like this: "Branding is about creating and sustaining trust, which means delivering on promises. The best and most successful brands are completely coherent. Every aspect of what they do and what they are reinforces everything else."

This kind of radical congruency where your values, words, and actions match is essential for building trust. Simply being consistent reflects integrity, which communicates credibility, authority, and authenticity. This in itself meets one of the most prevalent human needs: certainty.

Don Peppers and Martha Rogers made this point in their book *Extreme Trust: Honesty as a Competitive Advantage.* It has proven to be an incredible guide for building a foundation of trustability—an asset to sustainable ROI. In an interview with Charles Green, one of the authors of *The Trusted Advisor*, Don elaborated:

> The basic ethos governing all human social interaction contains a very strong requirement for trustability. The simple trustworthiness of your statements and actions, as an individual (or as a company or governmental organization), is a key attribute—the key attribute— in how your interactions will be interpreted, understood, and acted on by others. The social bond that connects us with others—the fuel that generates our collective intelligence and powers all our cultural and technological development—is based on trustability. As a result, the biggest single driver of the increased demand for trustability is today's rapid increase in the capability of interactive

technology, leading to a more and more connected and interactive human race.[10]

What does this mean for you? Building trust is critical to building your brand, your sales, and your Groundswell. The world demands it.

---

[10] Charles H. Green, "Don Peppers and Martha Rogers: Customer Trust Is the Next Big Thing (Trust Quotes #12)," Trusted Advisor, September 8, 2010, https://trustedadvisor.com/trustmatters/don-peppers-and-martha-rogers-customer-trust-is-the-next-big-thing-trust-quotes-12.

BUILDING AND ELEVATING TRUST

*"Making promises and keeping them is
a great way to build a brand."*

—Seth Godin

Luckily, building trust is as simple as making a promise and following through with it. Doing this time after time demonstrates a pattern others can rely on. Each time you prove them right, you build more trust. The more they learn who you are, the more you earn their trust. This culture of trust is built from three underlying fundamentals.

KNOW YOUR PROMISE

Your promise is the beating heart of your Groundswell and requires a solid handle on the two kinds of value:

- your foundational values (the foundation your business is built upon; what you stand for)
- your delivered value (the good or service you give to your audience that meets a specific need)

For your *values* and *value* to captivate your audience, they should be simple, credible, unique, memorable, and inspiring. This is what makes your promise worth believing—and investing—in.

Your promise both directly and indirectly communicates your mission, aka your Epic Outcome. This could be anything from advocating for recycling or fighting child labor to guaranteeing high-quality goods—but *something* must matter to you.

The more internal clarity you have for your Epic Outcome, the more clearly you will be able to communicate your mission, your *values and value*, and the promise you are making. Knowing and showing this with crystal clarity is precisely what will inspire others to align with you, trust you, and be led by you.

Without a clear promise, you risk lingering unnoticed, being forgotten, or being easily replaced by a competitor. In fact, many worthy audiences would pay a higher price to have something meaningful they can connect their own values to rather than be left unfulfilled. If you don't position yourself as having a clear mission—a stance on a topic, issue, or cultural movement—you don't actually have anything meaningful to promise. Without that foundation, it's impossible to build trust. Remember, without trust, your Groundswell will never exist.

In author Israelmore Ayivor's words: "Take a stand; go for the right choice. Don't just sit for anything; stand for something. Be specific, because sometimes, when the meaning is not clear, there is absolutely no meaning!"

Ask yourself: what is my company absolutely unwilling to bend on under any circumstances?

Whatever your answer is, lean into that—hard. More than one aspect may come to mind, but there will be a point of view that can and will connect to your core audience.

Communicate Your Promise

Clarity is key. Even if your promise is clear to you, if it's not communicated clearly to others, then it's all for naught. Communicating your values with transparency from your unique point of view is a simple way to treat people as humans. It gives them a choice. They can decide if they align or not. Problems arise when your communication is unclear.

Messaging that is vague or contradictory doesn't allow your audience to form a clear picture of who you are and what is different about you. This, in turn, makes them wary or apathetic about connecting with you. No one wants to follow or be part of a community if they are unsure what it stands for. Vague messaging will undermine your ability to win buy-in from your audience, and your Groundswell will stop before it even has a chance to begin. Author Joe Duncan rightly says, "Make your intentions clear; the universe does not respond well to uncertainty."

Intentionally create emotional, rational, and value connections that clarify your unique differentiator and express what is important to you.

Do this in *all* aspects of your messaging, everything from internal communications to marketing campaigns.

Don't hold back.

Be explicit about what you stand for.

Openly share your point of view so that those who align with you will recognize you. In fact, when you do, even those who don't align with you will appreciate your clarity. It's better to be obviously out of alignment than it is to present a shadowy view of what you're all about.

Additionally, make sure your audience has a clear way to *demonstrate* their alignment. Often, they may want to be involved but don't know how. Alignment does not have to look like a transaction —if a transaction is the only avenue you offer for audience engagement, you're missing out on the relational connection necessary for trust.

Get creative and make it easy for your audience to communicate with you and share their feedback. If your entire sales journey is automated, for example, make sure there's an easy way for people to voice their challenges or praise. Internally, designate someone in your organization to be responsible for providing key team members with updates on how the organization is connecting to and conversing with community, audience, and stakeholders. Active listening and responding is a key component to fostering trust, both inside and outside your organization.

Open and clear lines of communication build trust, making your audience much more likely to support you, share your messages, and help you build your Groundswell.

Deliver on Your Promise

This is the moment you've been waiting for: when your audience recognizes you and responds. Every interaction with your audience matters. Every interaction is a chance to deliver—or not deliver—on your promise.

You may have great customer service policies on paper, but if you don't live out the policies in spirit and action, they might as well be lies as far as your audience is concerned. In 2017, United Airlines learned this lesson the hard way. As The New York Times headline put it, "United Airlines Passenger Dragged from Overbooked Flight." One employee's misjudgment broke the trust of the public, leading to a backlash and massive impact on United's business. United Airlines only made this worse by downplaying the incident and praising its staff for following protocols. This immediately demonstrated a misalignment of values with their passengers.

The debacle wiped out $1.4 billion in value in a matter of hours. A second apology arrived, admitting that the incident was "truly horrific," but it was too late. The public damage was already done.

Most corrosions of trust will not be this overt or well-documented. In fact, they often go unnoticed, or pop up here and there. The very nature of high-volume human interactions creates risk for trust to deteriorate if left unchecked and unexamined. But no matter how small or how few and far between, every broken promise erodes trust.

A more mundane but relatable example is a business that has a policy of accepting returns but a reputation for making the customer feel like a criminal when they do return a purchase. Whether I'm returning a TV at the big-box store or a burger at the local diner, if I receive sighs of annoyance and a dismissive shrug, the interaction is wrecked. They've lost my trust. Not only am I less likely to visit that establishment again, but I am also going to share my experience with others. The *way* a business accepts returns matters just as much—and likely more than—whether they choose to take returns at all.

When I am received with empathy—when I am heard, understood, and accommodated, rather than being made to feel awkward or embarrassed—I'm going to walk away feeling amazing. Being valued and cared for is a completely different experience, one

I'm likely to rave positively about to anyone who will listen. Your audiences' experiences, both positive and negative, become your brand's identity. It cannot be overstated that word of mouth has the power to make or break your Groundswell.

How can we ensure positive experiences that lead to positive word of mouth? Through authentic alignment across every aspect of your endeavor, including leadership, employees, partners, and community members. In other words, a culture of trust.

NEXT-LEVEL CULTURE

It should be clear at this point that you can't build a Groundswell alone—it demands connection to others. This connection originates from the inside out. It's an alignment within your business, first and foremost.

In the book *Principles: Life and Work*, Ray Dalio writes, "People who have shared values and principles get along. People who don't will suffer through constant misunderstandings and conflicts… Too often in relationships, people's principles aren't clear. This is especially problematic in organizations where people need to have shared principles to be successful."

Mindfully creating empathetic and caring policies and practices is a great first step, but they are brought to life and made real within an internal culture of empathy and care. In this way, your internal culture directly creates your external brand. Your promise can only be effectively delivered to your audience when every member of your team shares the same values and participates in their expression.

Build Your Crew

We all know brands that live and die by their culture, which is often what we love most about them. All culture starts at the top. Starbucks CEO Howard Schultz explains it this way: "Our mission statement about treating people with respect and dignity is not just words but a creed we live by every day. You can't expect your employees to exceed the expectations of your customers if you don't exceed the employees' expectations of management."

We are entering into a more conscious era of understanding that people's time and commitment are vital, and that management should be there to support the culture, rather than the other way around. Today's workforce wants more than to trade time for money. They want leadership to have a clear and meaningful purpose behind where the company is going so they can be bought-in and aligned. This empowers them to show up with genuine empathy and care for your audience.

Just like the audience you want to serve, your employees are people with human needs, too. More often, today's employees are not looking to management to be "the man in charge," but rather for well-rounded support so they can not only be of better service to the humans that the business is trying to help, but also be able to experience a better, fuller, more fulfilled life as humans themselves.

They're tired of spending their precious minutes doing work that doesn't make an impact. They're tired of being treated like they're replaceable. They are hungry for meaningful contribution. This growing need is changing the way employees view their employers, and what employers need to demonstrate to attract staff.

That cultural shift is priming minds and paving the way for Groundswell culture.

Now with the gig economy and the ability to work remotely, it's even more important to incentivize through culture. People have more power to self-select where they work and are more likely to stay because they are *aligned*, not because it's hard to leave. If your business isn't delivering a culture that makes employees and contractors feel highly valued and a part of something that matters, you're unlikely to keep them.

With this in mind, VaynerMedia has designated a role of Chief Heart Officer. The person who fills that position, Claude Silver, described her role to *Forbes* like this:

> I oversee all of the people and their experience within the walls of Vayner. Some people might call me a Chief People Officer, some might say Chief HR Officer, but I don't say either of those. I really say Heart because I believe that human beings are full of heart. And every now and then, especially in corporate cultures, we end up forgetting that

part. So, my job is to oversee and work for 800 people, taking care of whatever their needs are, be that learning and development, growth, shifting teams, personal coaching, mental health issues, meditation, issues with managers, giving feedback, so forth, and so on.[11]

Gary Vaynerchuk's goal is to create a reason why their people will want to stay. He's investing in longevity by investing in culture. Yes, the expense of turnover is high, but it's more than just keeping the office full of warm bodies. It's about ensuring that the *best* people stick around, not just the most loyal.

If you can build a positive and supportive culture within your business that is based on positive core values, your employees become your biggest asset for marketing. Nothing is more powerful for your business than great interactions with your audience. This ultimately comes down to your employees. Honor this truth. Commit to creating a culture that highly serves the ones who serve your audience. One that meets them where they are, encourages them to grow, and incentivizes them to stay. Devote resources and thoughtful leadership to continually understand and support their needs.

---

[11] Andy Molinsky, "A Master Class in Emotional Intelligence from Gary Vaynerchuk's Chief Heart Officer Claude Silver," *Forbes*, May 21, 2019, https://www.forbes.com/sites/andymolinsky/2019/05/21/a-master-class-in-emotional-intelligence-from-gary-vaynerchuks-chief-heart-officer-claude-silver/.

At the end of the day, every employee is marketing your brand. The service they provide, the word of mouth they create, has the capacity for impact far greater than any ad spend.

Partnership Culture

By partnerships we're talking about the variety of lateral relation-ships that help you and your business thrive, from service part-ners and suppliers to peer networks, mentorships, and alliances. Fostering peer-to-peer and business-to-business relationships that align with your vision and goals can create mutually beneficial growth and sustainability.

Like your employees, your service partners and suppliers are also part of your culture and contribute to how you serve your audience. Partner relationships are fostered through authenticity, transparency, and generosity, not quid pro quo. If they are part of your ecosystem, they are part of your sustainability strategy, and you need to build goodwill and equity with them. A thriving partnership culture is a chance for operations to really shine. But transforming suppliers into partners requires a mindset shift, from demanding they conform to your wishes to inspiring them to join your mission of service. It's not enough for suppliers to simply meet an agreement; they need to buy in.

This means appealing to your suppliers to connect with you in a more intimate way. It's not enough to have a relationship with a supplier's salesperson; extend the connection to the most senior level possible, from leadership to leadership. Have a conversation that touches on process, prices, and people. Make a real effort.

Start by identifying concerns that are purely transactional. How reliant is your business on a particular supplier? Can they grow with you? What would happen if they went away? Do you need to diversify? Or are you so connected that you can feel confident they will deliver the same "brand promise" you are passing to your audience?

The Inner Circle—Community Culture

We've talked about internal culture (your team, crew, and staff) and external culture (your partners and suppliers), but there is a third layer of culture to consider: your community culture. It could be a group that you create, partner with, or support, but the alignment becomes an extension of your internal culture into an external community. It is another avenue where you can demonstrate your values and your value, creating visibility, credibility, and loyalty.

The concept of creating community culture is not new, but it's important to understand the impact and not simply view it as a "tactic" for good PR. You may have heard of the term "green washing," where businesses seem to invest in or support an eco-initiative only in order to add it to their "look, we did this" box as if it makes an impact. In fact, it does the opposite. An audience can see through it in a heartbeat; the company actually loses credibility and loyalty.

Community culture must not only align with your vision and values but be something that you hope will have an impact on the world. We are talking about genuine integration into your business where the intention is about making a positive impact on the world, not just the bottom line.

A Groundswell Parable:
Soulful Strategies

In the previous chapter, Koa and Kalani recognized the value of direct connection with their audience. Every day, Koa would hold court with visitors as he shaped boards. Their shop became a hot spot with members of the surf community, young and old stopping by to be part of the conversation. Alongside Koa's one-of-a-kind boards, Kalani strategically added supplemental merchandise—apparel and gifts made from recycled ocean plastic, not to mention wetsuits and other surf essentials from Koa's favorite brands.

Every person who entered the shop was treated like a precious natural resource, with love and respect and a desire to see them thrive in their chosen habitat.

And it worked! Just by being true to themselves and giving their best into the world, their business grew naturally and organically. When you have something good to offer the world, people are going to want it!

Increased business meant the work outpaced what two siblings could accomplish on their own. It soon became time to bring in others to help with the front end, leaving Kalani free to work on the business rather than in it all the time. And they found an apprentice or two to help Koa on the production side.

As business ramped up, they needed to make sure their primary value + values didn't get lost in the shuffle. In fact, during times of growth, your values and culture are more important than ever. The consistency of your internal culture creates trust. And when you do it right, your values and culture may even become the things your audience loves most about you. They want to stand with you because of what you stand for.

After working to create connection and establish value-based relationships with their audience, Koa and Kalani recognized the need to keep that vibe going across every aspect of their business. So, Koa and Kalani mentored the new employees closely to ensure they aligned and adhered to the values of the shop that were so primal to the brand and identity they had built. It took a little more time upfront, but Koa and Kalani believed it was worth it.

And it is. The primary goal as Koa and Kalani grow is to maintain the level of personal and integrity-driven service the shop is known for, so they can do more good in the world they love.

WAVES UPON WAVES

"Success is like a snowball...
It takes momentum to build, and the more you
roll in the right direction, the bigger it gets."

—Steve Ferrante, CEO of Champions

When you create connections across your entire brand, everyone—from your audience to your employees to your vendor partners to your community—can become wholeheartedly bought-in. That is precisely what we're building toward. Energy in a sustained direction over a period of time, like storm winds moving in the same direction, gives ample opportunity for waves to grow and gain momentum.

Momentum is easy to maintain but takes more energy to initiate.

SPINNING PLATES VERSUS PUSHING DOMINOS

The hyper world of "build fast" and short-term thinking makes uncommitted leaders change their plans like some people change socks. The days of irrelevant and interruptive marketing are over. The days of casting a wide net to catch anything and everything at the bottom of the sea are over. Those tactics amount to nothing more than spinning plates. Sure, you can start spinning plates immediately, but it requires you to keep spinning them and never stop. If people do not understand your promise, believe it, and see how it will lead to an exciting future for them, it will be impossible for them to align. The frantic effort becomes unsustainable fatigue.

Groundswelling, on the other hand, can be as effortless as pushing over dominoes—with effects that are just as far-reaching. With focus and intention, you take your time to set up all the pieces. Once the Build phase is completed, you just tip and watch momentum do the rest, carrying you all the way to your Epic Outcome. The moment doesn't happen by accident—it's intentionally built, with more time (patience), less friction (connection), and the unseen pull of gravity (trust). With these in place, momentum is not far behind.

Behind each wave is another set of waves until the progressive momentum of your Groundswell can't be stopped. Remember, just because the results may initially be unseen or small doesn't mean that you are not moving in the right direction.

Now, built on a foundation made to last, you're ready to tip the domino on the next phase: Give.

GIVE

GIVE IS THE NEW GET

"No one has ever become poor by giving."

—Anne Frank

Something special happens when we give. Think of something as simple as giving a smile to a stranger walking down the street. Try it. You will likely get a smile returned. If you choose to keep it to yourself, you might walk around all day without seeing someone smile at you. But if you initiate the smile—if you give *first*—you can and eventually will receive a smile and maybe more in return.

You know the truth of this simple act of giving. You've heard it and experienced it in one way or another your whole life. Albert Einstein once said, "The value of a man resides in what he gives." The Bible says, "It is more blessed to give than to receive."

Deepak Chopra echoed these principles when he said, "The universe operates through dynamic exchange… Giving and receiving are different aspects of the flow of energy in the universe. And in our willingness to give that which we seek, we keep the abundance of the universe circulating in our lives."[12]

The consistent thread of these teachings is that when you give, you set into motion an invisible dynamic that cannot help but come back to you, and you benefit from the intentional act of giving first. You initiate the energy with your act of giving, priming the pump so to speak, and it will flow back to you. This shift to giving first is foundational for creating a Groundswell.

What does it look like to flip from fishing for leads to investing in others?

Neil Patel is a shining example of this transformation. Patel is a *New York Times* bestselling author, top influencer, marketer,

---

[12] "The Law of Giving & Receiving," Chopra, May 26, 2015, https://chopra.com /articles/the-law-of-giving-receiving.

and creator of one of the one-hundred most brilliant companies according to *Entrepreneur* magazine. He is a monster content creator: his blog, podcast, and YouTube channel are consumed nearly twenty-five million times each month.

And he's also one of the most generous people in the digital marketing space. He gives away free content, training, and even software tools—the SEO tool that his competitors charge a hundred dollars a month to use, Neil gave away for free. Not only is he giving, but he's giving high value. His free marketing school content is better than most people's courses.

I recently had the pleasure of interviewing Neil, and I was in awe. [13] I asked him why he gives away all this amazing content, most of which is better than any book.

In response, Neil said, "The way I see it is if you give [things] away—and you demonstrate your capability and experience and value—then a certain percentage of people go, 'Well, you know this better than I do. I trust you. Why don't I just hire you?'"

Michael Brenner, a champion of the customer-centric approach to business, agrees: "The best content marketing is giving away

---

[13]   Scott A. Martin, "Neil Patel | Karma Marketing," June 17, 2019, in *Groundswell Origins*, podcast, 35:03, https://groundswellorigins.com/podcast/neil-patel.

your experience. Because, in fact, when you demonstrate your experience, it's an asset of the company that can be utilized over and over again." [14]

[14] Scott A. Martin, "Michael Brenner | Why Human Centric Content Marketing?" May 7, 2019, in *Groundswell Origins*, podcast, 1:06:57, https://groundswell origins.com/podcast/michael-brenner.

GIVING VALUE

The economics of Give still trip people up, so we need to break down why giving works—both in real life and on paper.

To begin, the very act of giving is underscoring your values. According to science that David Allison explains in *Valuegraphics*, it is your values, not your advertising money, that bring people in. When interviewed about his research and work around *Valuegraphics*, David explained:

> Neuroscientists will tell you that the prefrontal cortex…is the CEO of your brain, and that nothing happens in your body. You don't do anything or think anything until the CEO tells you that's what you're

going to do. And the CEO uses one thing to determine how it's going to react to any inputs coming into your system: your values.[15]

David's study validated the idea that people are not rational or emotional buyers. Ultimately, we are driven by what aligns to our values. This is great news! It frees you to attract both rational and emotional types, simply by being more authentically who you are. And so, if we really want to hit the mark and turn our Give into dollars, we must understand and declare our values as an intermingled part of that process.

Doing so begins with throwing out archaic marketing language. This may sound familiar, as we addressed the distinction between an "acquiring customers" mindset and a "connecting with people" mindset earlier in the book. In fact, each of the previous phases continues as before, as well as having additional layers of application. Another example is a concept we addressed in Build: we named identifying common values as one of the fastest ways to connect to others. Now, in Give, we can apply it in new ways to uncover our unique application.

---

[15] Scott A. Martin, "David Allison | Marketing Using Demographic Stereotypes Is Dead," July 5, 2020, in *Groundswell Origins*, podcast, 56:15, https://groundswellorigins.com/podcast/david-allison.

No matter what kind of business you're in, even a charitable organization, serving your audience requires an exchange of value. The value returned to you might be money, or it might be participation or feedback. Either way, this exchange is what business is all about. But before the exchange can ever happen, we have to get our audience on board with us. Before you can *get*, you need to *give* true value.

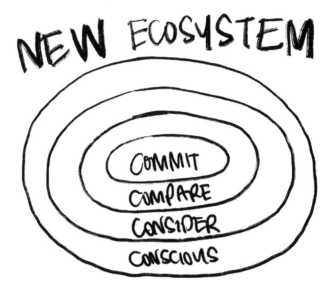

The modern audience is fluid. Today's modern human is different in every moment and wants to be interacted with as an individual. This kind of interaction requires removing linear thinking. Think instead of a ring; your audience enters and exits where and when they like, and your job is to generate pull, as with a magnetic tractor beam.

Let's look more closely at the typical sales funnel—that is, the key stages prospects move through before becoming your customer. It's most likely some version of the following:

1. **Consciousness:** Prospects become aware of you or what you offer. It enters their consciousness, often referred to as the awareness phase.

2. **Consideration:** Prospects gather enough information to ask themselves, "Is this for me? Do I need this now?"

3. **Comparison:** Before saying yes, prospects want to ensure they are making the right choice and will often weigh other options (i.e., competitors) to your offering.

4. **Commitment:** The prospect decides to buy with you. The level of commitment may vary, being anything from "I will buy in the future" to "I will buy right now," but at this point, they either "buy or buy in" or don't.

YOU HAVE TO DO THE (I) TO GET THE (R) IN ROI

Traditionally, businesses craft this journey by having the marketing department determine the cost of reaching and acquiring each customer across these four stages. In other words, how much does it cost to change a prospect from stranger to customer? And how much is gained when the prospect becomes a customer? This cost-of-acquisition ratio is a common tool for measuring profitability—and often, to make the most money, businesses only invest the minimum needed to acquire the customer. If you're a one-trick pony that just wants single-serve clients, this math may suit you fine. But if you're in business for return customers, the calculation is flawed.

In their book *Return on Customer*, Don Peppers and Martha Rogers go into great detail to help us understand the *total lifetime value* of our customers. Rather than thinking solely of the acquisition cost and initial return, this metric helps us understand the total potential value of customers over the average length of time they'll be with you. In an interview, Don offered this advice:

> The value of your customers is not a capital asset on your balance sheet. It's a fictional economic quantity that can exist, but it's not on your balance sheet. A lot of companies are simply strapped to the millstone of short-term results—"I've got to get short-term results for the shareholders or CFO"—and I would fault the accounting system for that.
>
> I tell companies, "If you think treating customers right and delivering a really good experience to them is costly, the only reason you think that is because you're working on the wrong timeframe."
>
> The truth is it's the most fruitful kind of investment you could possibly make, but the returns are in the future, not this quarter. It might cost you money today, but it's going to return many more times than that tomorrow.[16]

---

[16] Scott A. Martin, "Don Peppers | Trust Is the New Currency." January 6, 2020, in *Groundswell Origins*, podcast, 1:03:00, https://groundswellorigins.com /podcast/don-peppers.

THE BOTTOM LINE

Let's look at a tangible example of what this means. Let's say our average total lifetime value of a customer is $100, and the cost of acquiring them (moving them through the four phases of the acquisition funnel) is $20. From a traditional perspective, that's a profitable model. But what if you could increase their total lifetime value to $300? It might cost you more than $20 upfront—maybe it costs you $100. My argument is that we should be looking at what's possible long-term and investing more upfront to make it happen.

When you invest in giving upfront, and giving based on your values, you—like Neil Patel—change the game around customer acquisition. And then, when prospects do respond, you get good data about the future value of that customer. You can estimate their "total lifetime value" in the context of the value you've given them already, and what it cost you to do so.

In fact, when we give enough value out of the gate, we don't have to factor in the cost of multiple stages of the funnel. When your offer is captivating and irresistible enough, it can collapse the stages of a buyer's journey to move customers straight from Consideration to Commitment. Those are Groundswell results.

What would you be willing to invest in results like *that*?

GIVING ACROSS EVERY PHASE

"Every single interaction, the most minute detail of the interaction you have with your customer, is an opportunity for you to create something remarkable."

—Joey Coleman, Author, *Never Lose a Customer Again*

Instead of just looking at the literal steps your audience is taking and the cost to you at each point, let's revisit each one to find new opportunities to Give—to demonstrate value and values, and to contribute to the lifetime value of that customer.

Consciousness

Before they can become an active participant in your Groundswell, your audience needs to know who you are and what you offer. Your task here is to make them see you—and see you clearly.

At consciousness, either your audience recognizes that you can solve a problem for them or they're curious about whether you can. They're only willing to invest a bit—just a few moments to consider your offering.

Traditionally, most business owners create awareness through push marketing and advertising, which asks for business immediately and often prompts the audience with demands, like *Buy now!*

When you focus on giving value instead, you shift into *pull* marketing, which is softer and more attractive to customers. Once a person becomes aware of something of value, especially value that is a delight to receive, they will often share about it with others. This amplifies your ability to gain even more conscious awareness from them and the people around them.

If you want consciousness, give value that will naturally attract the attention needed.

Consideration

This second stage in the journey is when customers start to become more familiar with your good or service by evaluating you. They ask questions such as, *Is this worth my time? Can this help me? Is it relevant?*

At this important juncture, your audience is determining how beneficial you can be to them, and how simple or hard your good or service will be to use or leverage.

A company that immediately helps someone by giving value that meets a need—without asking for anything but consideration in return—frees the potential customer up to ask questions without feeling like they will be pressured into a commitment too soon.

Giving generously shortens the gap between consciousness and consideration without pushing your customer further than they're willing to go.

Comparison

At this stage, the customer investigates whether there is a good or service out there better than yours. Your audience is not just looking at what you have to offer, but also weighing it against the other options out there.

The great news is that by giving value, you have banked equity in the mind of the prospect; *and* you have stacked momentum, since they have already experienced some of what it's like to do business with you.

This equity and momentum builds an invisible barrier to entry for your competitor. Unless your competitor has also invested by giving value to the potential customer before purchase, the prospect likely can't help but lean toward you. They'll wonder how much value they'll get from you *after* a purchase, because they already got so much value beforehand!

Commitment

The customer's final decision is based on timing and how much confidence they have in what you are offering. What is compelling about buying your good or service *right now*? Most importantly: do they trust you to provide it?

This is the ultimate connection you're working toward. But be aware that commitment does not always translate into a sale. It could be simply a commitment to follow you or subscribe—these are both stages of commitment, and they each carry their own value. The more your audience interacts with you, the more they experience your value and values, and the more confident they'll feel about increasing their commitment over time.

It is possible for commitment to happen in one interaction. But, as with any relationship, reaching the commitment stage can take time and patience. Often, the bigger the commitment—especially when time, money, and needs are at stake—the slower your audience will move through these stages.

That's good news, though, because by the time they reach the commitment stage, after all that engagement, they haven't just bought—they have *bought in* to what sets you apart. Customers like this often become assets to your future growth through word of mouth and "superfan" behavior.

RETHINKING THE FUNNEL

Traditionally, acquisition is presented as a funnel, moving prospects linearly from one stage to the next, narrowing the walls on them until they drop into commitment. People, too, think about this process singularly. Most marketers just focus on "buy or go away," matching a stagnant offer with a targeted prospect. And they offer it in the same way every time: an explicit sales page that scrolls the prospect through four testimonials and five reasons why they should buy, then finally shows them the real offer—only to pull a classic infomercial trick *(But wait! There's more!)*. When people are in this kind of funnel, they know it—and they're not happy about it.

Now, don't get me wrong—the funnel isn't dead. There's nothing wrong with providing a sequence of information to help people make a decision. But the funnel *is* evolving.

Instead of trapping people, this system should give your audience access to valuable information in a beautiful way. Instead of being force-fed a good, potential customers can learn and engage when they're ready to.

We've already seen how giving real value, in a way that creates obligation without making our audience feel trapped, moves customers through that kind of funnel more effectively. Now we need to rethink the *way* we interact with our audience at each of those points. In other words, to generate a Groundswell, even a funnel has to give value.

Content marketing expert Ashley Faus says the funnel is outdated and suggests breaking free from it by thinking of it more like a playground that people interact with.[17] Rather than boxing people in, design content on a jungle gym that lets them explore and discover from different directions and in different ways. You're creating an ecosystem of value that your audience can interact with on their own terms and in their own time. This is how people want to experience and interact with content and brands.

---

[17] Scott A. Martin, "Ashley Faus | The New Buyer's Journey Is a Playground," February 5, 2021, in *Groundswell Origins*, podcast, 1:04:42, https://groundswell origins.com/podcast/ashley-faus.

When you give value in a way that feels like freedom, your value increases in the eyes of your audience. And your interactions take on a new dynamic—one that draws your audience in instead of pushing them away. In the context of building a Groundswell, a Give funnel starts with an invitation: *we are here to help and serve humans without trickery, misrepresentation, or bad intentions.* If you can add fun and playfulness into that experience, all the sweeter.

AN INVITATION TO GIVING MORE VALUE

In nature, hummingbirds are attracted to flowers because they hold delicious value. But you don't have to be a flower to get in on this game. You can also be a hummingbird feeder. Hummingbird feeders are manufactured value to hummingbirds, and the birds don't care! In fact, it turns out that a hummingbird is more attracted to a feeder than it is to a flower. The feeder is both sweeter and easier to access. Even in a sea of flowers, the hummingbird chooses the feeder.

Kelly Slater, eleven-time world surfing champion, has manufactured a wave that's consistent and reoccurring *and* he loves surfing natural waves; in fact, my guess is that he prefers natural. I am sure both hummingbirds and humans prefer natural—but can also enjoy manufactured when there is no natural option *or* when it can be delivered reliably, consistently, and at the same standard.

Three Steps to Giving

This is how you should think of Giving—and of marketing overall. You're not trapping your audience in a net. You're not holding them down in a cage. You're just giving. You're inviting them to be delighted and rewarded.

These three steps—Invite, Delight, and Reward—are the framework you can use at every point along the journey with your audience, whether you use a funnel or a playground. They show you *how* to Give.

Invite

An invitation is different from an ask. An invitation feels special and has an element of exclusivity and excitement. It feels good right away. This is the first subtle, but vital, approach to an impactful Give. Invite your audience to share and connect with your value and values, then give them options about what to do next.

As we've discussed, don't use the old funnel mentality of one obvious and expected choice—this isn't "buy or go away." But also, beware of offering too many choices that overwhelm your audience. Create your invitation with a gentle off-ramp to a secondary (and maybe tertiary) choice.

Delight

Now it's time to delight your audience with something unexpected. What feeling do you want them to have? Whatever you deliver needs to generate that experience in a way that surpasses their expectations or imagination. Surprise them, maybe more than once, with the feeling they are experiencing in this moment or what they will experience by accepting the invitation.

Reward

There are many great companies who stop there and do see growth, but when pursuing a Groundswell, we're looking to grow exponentially. To anchor and transform the connection you've made, next reward your audience for taking action. I'm not talking about a monetary or savings reward, but something that is experiential, meaningful, congruent, personalized, and relevant. Make them feel how much you care and how grateful you are that they're part of your movement.

Imagine if Invite, Delight, Reward was the standard for how you interacted with your prospects and customers across every portion of the relationship. When you embrace that—from consciousness to commitment and beyond—you create something that is harder to say no to than to say yes. Tony Robbins describes this as an "irresistible offer."

IRRESISTIBLY VALUABLE

While you may be unlocking your own joy through this Give-fest, there is a catch: giving-to-get is not a huge secret. All your competitors know about it, too. There is more free "helpful content" available now than ever before. How often do you get asked for your email in order to gain access to an eBook or some other valuable, gated content? This onslaught of offers can be overwhelming for givers and receivers alike.

We're all tired of selling and being sold to—and we may be approaching a time when we're tired of being *given* to as well. And yet, giving is still the answer. The key is that your Give cannot be shallow. It must provide deep value—and be something that only you can give.

Your irresistible offer should not only demonstrate the value you provide, but should also directly impact the values you hold. Alignment between who you are and what you're giving is essential. When you combine the powerhouses of value and values, you share a truth about who you really are and give customers an opportunity not just to buy, but to buy into what you're all about.

A highly differentiated or personalized Give is a significant part of making your offer irresistible *and* making it valued.

This is how you craft *your* irresistible offer.

Give Is a Pull, Not a Push

Like the ocean's tides, your people are drawn to you. The moon doesn't convince, cajole, or beg the tide. Gravity is simply the moon's natural attractive state. When you find the right offer, you will know it. It's like finding gravity between the moon and the tide.

In this way, your Give becomes a magnet.

Let's say a plumber is looking for ways to connect with people in their service area. They experiment with a Give by donating to a clean water nonprofit for every new connection their customers create for them. It's a nice offer, and may even feel close to a personal value that the plumber holds. But it doesn't connect the plumber's value to the individual. When they change their offer to a free at-home water testing kit, it aligns their value of providing safe, clean, functioning water with the very service they provide in a way that is irresistible to their ideal customer.

Your Give doesn't have to look like what you might expect. Think outside of the discount box here, because even your business model can be a method for giving. A social enterprise, for example, is all about creating a Groundswell around a cause, but within a for-profit model. While all businesses will need Give as part of their journey, the structure of a social enterprise anchors this into its very foundation. Deciding whether use this model to make an impact would be part of your Build phase. Then you'd share this aspect of who you are and what you're all about in the Give phase as a way to communicate your values.

A great Give sets your values in motion. What can you give— joyfully—to show people the value you have to offer, rooted in the values that drive your business model?

Answering that question will reveal your best method of giving.

If you can't identify your values, go back to Build. And if you're not sure what value will delight and reward your audience, take some time to identify and meet their needs.

Focus Your Give

"*Trying to appeal to everyone is almost sure to fail,
for the simple reason that everyone
wants something different!*"

—Seth Godin

Creating a Groundswell is not about attracting *everyone*. Remember, a Groundswell moves in one direction, so your Give should be focused on those who align with what you're building. If they don't align but you try to reach them anyway, you'll end up watering down what you're doing to make it palatable or more broadly irresistible.

A contest to win a million dollars is likely to bring in your audience, sure, but it will also bring in everyone else. This can be costly, distracting, and—ultimately—a big miss.

Your value and values are too awesome to get lost in the noise of generic offerings. Instead, focus your Give so that it's uber attractive to *your* hummingbirds. If other birds choose to roll up and enjoy the nectar, that's fine—but a Groundswell grows when you're building for and giving to your core audience.

That is what a Groundswell is all about: connecting to a concentrated, core, Epic Center of energy that's created from a core audience. You don't need the people who don't get it. You only need the people who do. When that core audience reaches critical mass, it begins expanding to the point that it becomes a sustainable ecosystem.

Now that we know you can and should limit your audience, you have to determine whether your Give idea is a good fit for your specific Groundswell momentum.

Cool as ICE

Sean Ellis is considered the godfather of growth hacking and created a decision matrix to help identify the most valuable approaches to Give, from marketing experiment to the most effective offer. It's called ICE, which stands for Impact-Confidence-Ease. You can apply ICE to offers, campaigns, and experiments—and when "The Give" is slightly complex, like offering an additional service that requires multiple stakeholders and considerations.

Let's walk through the process.

1. First, brainstorm all the ways you could possibly show your value to your core audience. List whatever crazy thing you think of—nothing is off limits.
2. Next, step back and look at it more objectively through the ICE lens. Create a grid with your ideas on one axis and I, C, and E on the other axis.
3. Evaluate the merit of each idea by considering its ICE on a scale of one to ten, with one being the lowest and ten being the highest. Take your best guess and rate each

factor individually for each idea, creative program, or marketing campaign.

I is for impact. How much will executing this idea move the needle for my brand, vision, goals, and ultimate end? Little to no impact (1), an exponential amount of impact (10), or some gradient in between?

C is for confidence. How confident am I that I can execute this idea? Have I done this before successfully? Are there case studies demonstrating how other people did this, or is it something new and untried? Little to no confidence (1), extreme confidence (10), or some gradient in between?

E is for ease. How easy is the process to execute this idea? Does it require new software? New programs and campaigns? How many resources and variables? Not easy (1), very easy (10), or some gradient in between?

Rate each factor individually and then come up with a total to determine which ideas have the highest scores.

This is not an exact science but is meant to give you a better indication of a "hell yes" versus a "hell no." But even when you total the scores, the answer will rarely be a direct *yes* or *no*, a *do it* or a *don't*. This is about prioritization.

Different Gives will impact different goals and aspects of your strategy. For example, one goal might be to get a thousand subscribers, while another might be to increase sales for a specific good or service. These are both goals you want to pursue, so it's a matter of prioritization and understanding which Give best fits with each outcome. Then it's up to you to decide what action to take based on your goals and the ICE factor.

Chris More, a highly respected strategist who led growth for the FireFox browser, came up with his own iteration. He added a fourth letter—R for Reach, replacing ICE with RICE.[18] Reach is about how many people are conscious of the offering, following through, and connecting. Reach is important for outbound marketing strategies—you can measure it by tracking which campaign was received by each person and whether they responded. This gives you even more information to make future decisions. Chris explains:

> You may have a high-impact idea, but it may only reach a small amount of people. But you can have the inverse of that: an idea that has a small impact, but the reach is really big. Utilizing RICE instead of ICE allows you to balance out your serviceable market for

---

[18] Scott A. Martin, "Chris More | Sustainable Growth through Innovation," June 11, 2020, in *Groundswell Origins*, podcast, 1:14:56, https://groundswellorigins .com/podcast/chris-more.

whatever the idea is… When I'm doing a RICE prioritization, I look at the relationship between [Reach] and [Impact] together.[19]

Regardless of the outcome of RICE, the simple act of pausing to think about your offering in this context allows you to maximize it in a way that will further your goals for Groundswell. It's an important consideration and a great innovation.

---

[19] Ibid.

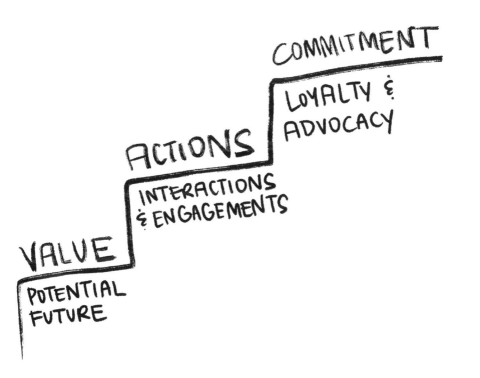

LEVEL UP YOUR GIVE

Giving isn't a one-time thing. It's an indispensable piece of your Groundswell and a means of sharing value that you hold dearly and believe in. Giving is ongoing and occurs at every stage of the relationship. But that doesn't mean your Give will look the same for everyone you serve at all times. We know that different people have different lifetime values for your brand and bring that value at different stages in their relationship with you. This presents an opportunity to Give to each person uniquely.

You can determine the level of your Give based on three things:

1. their value—potential future value
2. their actions—interactions and engagements
3. their commitment—when someone has already bought from you

Each customer's needs are different based on their engagement cycle, but some customers are of higher influence and could impact more people through their interactions with you. Subscribers, followers, and paying loyal clients each have a different level of commitment and, therefore, potential value.

While you want your audience to experience the value you give early in the process, be careful. If you frontload too much and don't keep adding value as you continue to serve them, it feels like any other company that only gives value at the start. Consider cable TV companies, for example. They give new customers all kinds of value just for signing up, but after an initial period, all that stops. This is a common problem for marketing departments because they are overly obsessed with acquisition, which can backfire later in the relationship. When the Give decreases over time, it incentivizes customers to leave. To build a successful Groundswell, you want your audience to feel that the longer they are with you, the more value they experience, which will most certainly deepen their commitment.

Just as frontloading can become a problem, there is a caution on the other side, as well. Even in committed and loyal relationships, it's vital that the information gained not be misused to hold people hostage. If not handled with care, a cumulative Give can demote your relationships to transactions. Take airline miles, for example. They create a Give that encourages increased commitment: the more you fly, the more miles you earn, and the more flights you can take. But if the service doesn't carry the same value and create a delightful experience, then my view of them will only lessen over time. I may still fly with Airline A because of the miles, but I'd be choosing them begrudgingly, not enthusiastically. This trapped feeling does not lead to positive word of mouth and can ultimately erode the relationship. When Airline B comes along offering triple miles to switch, I will happily jump ship because Airline A hasn't cultivated an emotional relationship with me.

When someone experiences real value, they don't have to be convinced or hassled to stick around—they choose to stay. And that is empowering, for your customers and for you. When you give the freedom to go but the true value necessary to stay, you earn the deepest levels of commitment. Remember: your offer (what you give) should always demonstrate and align with your value and values.

GIVE DOESN'T MEAN FREE

"Free" is one of the most popular words to people's ears.

Let's be clear: when it comes to building a Groundswell, *Give* doesn't mean giving away the farm. It doesn't even have to be free—although it can be if that makes sense for your situation.

Give doesn't have to be an economic offering at all, such as a discount or sale. Giving can simply be a way for people to get insight into your magic or to connect with your values. It's an offer your audience can accept or not, and while it *can* be free, a Give isn't *required* to be free for the principle to work. You get to decide what receiving extreme value will be like for your customer—even if it still requires something of them.

People buy on value, but they *buy in* when you share values alongside the value you're offering.

For example, the "freemium" model is where you give a portion or a taste of your product or service for free to let people get a sense of your offering. This cost of giving it away is offset by offering an upgrade at a premium where you recoup your loss. It's a fair exchange, because if they don't see the value, why upgrade? If you give too much away and don't demonstrate your continued or value-added offering, it can be a very costly strategy.

In the end, it's giving first so people "buy in." When you're trying something unconventional or you want to pull people in to just experience what you have, this can be an incredibly powerful way to do it. You have reduced their risk and offset your customer acquisition costs of attracting people to buy.

In a Groundswell, we're talking about giving something beyond the freemium level. It's not just a giveaway. It can be an offer, extending your hand to meet your audience halfway, or giving them additional support or value around the good or service they purchased.

It's the subtle difference between, "Here's this tool to use for free" and "Here's this tool; let me show you how to use it. In fact, I'll help you use it, as far as I can from an economic perspective.

And, hey, if you want to pay me to use it for you, just give me a call."

I have heard a saying: "The bigger the transaction, the bigger the transformation," and it might be worth considering. The more commitment you get from your audience through their sharing of information and investing into your offering—while getting an irresistible offer—the more likely they will be to "buy in."

A Groundswell Parable:
Scale Your Growth

From winning the contest to opening their own storefront and bringing on support staff, Groundswell Goods gained publicity and momentum that led to stable revenue and comfortable operations. Because of this, Kalani was able to shift her focus from daily operations to long-term strategy, and she decided it was time to leverage more of their number one asset: Koa's surfing knowledge and captivating presence.

Along with the online video content Kalani had been capturing of Koa in the workshop, where he waxed philosophic as he waxed boards, the two of them decided it was time to host a grand opening and roll out their Irresistible Offer (Give) in order to acquire sales and new contacts. The siblings recognized that giving value is essential and wanted to do something to invigorate their community and sow into the next generation of surfers, so they decided to give *big:* they offered free surf sessions to anyone who was needing first-time help.

The result was even bigger than they'd expected. This turned out to be a double-edged sword. Their target audience response was amazing, with people figuratively lined up around the block booking lessons; but because Koa and Kalani didn't anticipate such a large response, they didn't have the infrastructure in place to handle it well. This cost them dearly, as some people had to wait so long for a lesson that they went elsewhere or just lost enthusiasm for their decision to accept the invitation. To salvage the effort, Kalani and Koa had to cut off the promotion earlier than intended so they could fulfil their commitments in a timely manner.

In the aftermath, they realized their mistake and returned to their Build mindset so they could better prepare for the response from their audience. They did so many things right—right values, right intention—but their Give did not match their infrastructure so was a faulty execution. A big oops that they can learn from and then Give again, better than ever.

WHEN GIVING LEADS
TO GETTING

"There is one word which may serve as a rule of practice for all one's life: reciprocity."

Confucius

Giving value early is like sowing a seed; it's an investment for future harvest. You're giving to give but that doesn't mean you won't *also* get. It turns out, reciprocity is human nature. World-class negotiator Jeff Cochran once told me, "When people give, the other side immediately feels a compelling need to give something back."

This seemingly simple concept of Give is a critical component to getting momentum started in a Groundswell. You can't create a wave of marketing potential without it.

We're tied to one another and, like it or not, we all intrinsically keep score. When someone receives, a hidden force of obligation occurs, one they likely don't even recognize they have. They feel compelled to either pay it back or pay it forward. Either way, giving leads to more giving, and inevitably to more getting.

A recipient is more likely to experience the subtle obligation of reciprocity when what they receive has value.

But don't think of this obligation as anything other than value returned. This is a good thing! When what you've given is worthwhile—it's authentic to you, aligned with your mission, and adds to the recipient's life—what could possibly be bad about getting in return? Even if someone doesn't accept your offer, let alone reciprocate, you're still sowing consciousness for the future. As long as you offer value that aligns with your values, you can't lose.

THE RULES OF RECIPROCITY

During my interview with Jeff Cochran, we discussed Robert B. Cialdini's book *Influence: The Psychology of Persuasion*, in which he provides examples of this reciprocity in action.[20] In one experiment, Cialdini and his team sent out a large volume of holiday greeting cards to people they didn't actually know and ended up receiving a large response of return holiday cards.

Even though the card recipients were chosen at random and had no direct connection to the senders, when people received a holiday card, their sense of obligation prompted them to send one in return.

With this in mind, Jeff encouraged listeners to give value in a way they can leverage:

> It's in knowing the people that we're dealing with. Sometimes it's thoughtfulness. Here's an article that I thought you might be interested in. Here are some free samples of those items that you showed interest in. Whatever it might be to set up that sense of obligation … People do not like to leave their accounts unsettled. When you

---

[20] Scott A. Martin, "Jeff Cochran | Mastering Negotiations & Influence," September 8, 2019, in *Groundswell Origins*, podcast, 59:02, https://groundswellorigins.com/podcast/jeff-cochran.

receive, you immediately have an impulse, a human impulse, to give back.

That means, not only should you give, but at this stage you can also ask:

> The best time to tap into that sense of applicant obligation is right after you've given something... Anytime we give someone something, they're right on the cusp of giving something back, so it's right to ask for it. It is an appropriate dance for it at that point.

But one warning: if your receiver feels that you are giving in order to get, the silent obligation isn't created and instead they will put up walls and reject you. How do we prevent this from happening? By always ensuring that our Give is high value to our audience. In fact, when you are giving something that is painful for you— something you feel like you probably should be charging for— then you know it's at a good level. This pang is the signal that you're at the beginning of giving.

Then your next step is to ensure that you have created a way to receive. Create an avenue for them to give back to you. This is another opportunity to invoke Invite, Delight, Reward—with a call to action or a way for your recipients to show their commitment. If you're giving but not including a chance for them to give back to you, you're actually depriving them of additional value.

Because it truly is better to give than to receive—even for your audience.

Tapping into the art of Giving, knowing it will *likely* lead to getting but also releasing the expectation or even the anticipation of it, creates so much freedom for both the giver and receiver. In his book *Influence: The Psychology of Persuasion*, Cialdini translates the principles of giving and receiving as also being those of persuasion:

- **Reciprocity**—people are more likely to do something in return of a favor, regardless of the favor done and the ask now presented to them.
- **Commitment and Consistency**—people who have taken one action are likely to take another, regardless of the size or difference in action.
- **Social Proof**—in a state of uncertainty, people look to the actions of others to help them make their own decisions.
- **Authority**—people look to those in positions of authority to decide which actions to take.
- **Liking**—people will do business more readily with people and companies they like than with those they don't like or are indifferent to.
- **Scarcity**—people will take action when they are worried that they will miss out on the opportunity in the future.

When you leverage the principles of influence and reciprocity by Giving, you optimize the traditional acquisition funnel. You also collapse the time and energy (not to mention the cost) of the entire sales journey through persuasion without pressure.

Focusing on what you can give your audience that will demonstrate your value and values changes the funnel from a *push to get* into a *pull with give*, inviting connection and building trust with the very people you wish to serve.

In other words, the key to getting is to be a giving human. Give is the new get. Thoughtful generosity activates a boomerang effect of reciprocity that can transform incredible gifts into exceptional results.

So give, give, give—and don't give up. You're well on your way to generating your Groundswell. This is the primer to getting the momentum you need to start *getting* results.

THE POWER OF GIV

THE ONGOING POWER OF GIVE

*"Gratitude is what starts the
receiving process."*

—Jim Rohn

By giving value, you become an agent of change in the lives of
your audience and invite them to participate in generating a new
economy—one driven by value. Your Irresistible Offer becomes
a magnet that attracts your core audience to you, inviting them
to be delighted and rewarded for their commitment. This level of
giving leads to getting—more referrals, more loyalty, and more
return on the investment of your gift.

To keep the original spirit of the Give in place once the getting
begins, don't forget to embed mindfulness, graciousness, and gratitude into your process. I am always impressed with businesses
that go to great lengths to thank me for their business—whether
they do so immediately, intermittently, or in an ongoing fashion.
This is how you treat your clients.

Your reputation and the effectiveness of your delivery will
determine how big your Groundswell will become. When customers feel cared for and appreciated, they feel part of your core,
your tribe. They feel like they belong. When people feel they've
found their place with your good or organization, they help

you find others like them to bring into the circle, as well. Help them help you! This is how to grow exponentially, naturally, and sustainably.

GROW

GROUNDSWELL IS THE NEW GROWTH

The time has come to talk about the reason you likely picked up this book in the first place—Growth.

But as you have seen, Groundswell growth is not like other growth. Pursing Groundswell growth quits the getting-as-big-as-you-can-as-fast-as-you-can game and instead seeks to provide as much value as possible for as long as possible. It's Growth that is truly beautiful to see.

Now you can see why we don't pursue Growth from the get-go. We can only approach Growth because of all the work that has been done in the previous phases. **Build** an epicenter of deep purpose, using the principles of the Build phase, *so you can* **Give** extreme value to attract your audience and serve them well, *so you can* **Grow** sustainably, *so you can* create an impact that lasts. Once you Build a foundation of patient strategy, human connection, and complete trust and Give your audience unique value in alignment with your values—once you've established your Build and offered your Give—you can set your sights on Grow. You've already worked to ensure that your goods, process, partners, and people are aligned and ready to scale. As you read on and find ways to scale, make sure everything you choose to do continues to build on the wave of potential you've already set in motion.

As we've lamented before, many businesses (and business books) skip the foundation and focus on Growth first, assuming that to keep up with competitors in the market they must urgently scale. It's easy to fall victim to this way of thinking—both the allure of perceived success and the fear of failure if you don't chase it. Not only does this lead you astray of your brand's true purpose, but the risks are real. An estimated 70 percent of companies don't make it past their tenth year.[21] Attempting Growth before you're ready will only do you harm. Businesses that do this end up one of two ways:

---

[21] Data from the US Bureau of Labor Statistics shows that approximately 20 percent of new businesses fail during the first two years of being open, 45 percent during the first five years, and 65 percent during the first ten years. Only 25 percent of new businesses make it to fifteen years or more. (Source: "Entrepreneurship and the U.S. Economy," U.S. Bureau of Labor Statistics, last updated April 28, 2016, https://www.bls.gov/bdm/entrepreneurship/bdm_chart3.htm.)

- like a wind swell where they fizzle out shortly because they lack the infrastructure to generate growth; or
- like a tsunami where they grow too big too fast and destroy the infrastructure they had built, sabotaging their sustainability—they might be growing now, but it's only a matter of time before it all comes crashing down.

A Groundswell is about more than the size of the balance sheet or quantity of transactions—it's about serving your audience well. This is precisely why we spend so much time on Build and Give. If not, the very act of pursuing Growth will damage your Groundswell. Thirty-three percent of Americans say they consider switching companies after just a single instance of poor service.[22] Seventy-four percent of people are likely to switch brands if they find the purchasing process too difficult.[23] When service fails, trust is eroded, connection is broken, and strategies fail.

Like an iceberg where the real size and magnitude is hidden, so is Groundswell Growth where the foundational work is below the surface. The visible Growth is just the tip; the real Growth is what you can't see.

---

[22] "American Express Global Customer Barometer 2017," American Express, https://business.americanexpress.com/sg/~/media/Files/GCP/sg2/business-trends-insights/Amex_GCSB_Infographics.pdf?la=en-GB.

[23] "State of the Connected Customer," Salesforce, https://www.salesforce.com/resources/research-reports/state-of-the-connected-customer/.

But lucky for us all, just as pursuing Growth without your foundation sabotages growth and sustainability, the opposite is also true. A foundation that serves your audience well can't help but grow. In either scenario, the outcome is inevitable.

GROWING NATURALLY

"Unwavering incremental change can create
remarkable and monumental results."

—Ryan Lilly

Growth doesn't have to look like a crazy ad campaign. In fact, in a Groundswell, you don't need to chase Growth at all. Natural growth is just you being you, leaning into your values and value. Organic connections spring up from the world around you in response to the way you show up and give. The more you focus on your value and values, and seek to communicate them as clearly as possible, the more your audience will buy in and grow.

It may take time for your audience to understand what you're doing and to believe in you. They may even have questions at first. But once they see that you're trustworthy and valuable, they will give their buy-in—and you will get Groundswell-worthy Growth.

ADD MASSIVE VALUE

Sometimes your value is obvious and ensures a direct connection to Growth. Sometimes your value and values are so great that ICE doesn't matter. That level of tenacity and genuine passion can often generate Growth in ways you could never predict. This is not a call to throw wisdom out the window, but to lean into your value above all else.

One of my favorite examples of natural growth comes from Tony Robbins. He details how a young new real estate agent in LA was trying to break into the community and get listings. He repeatedly tried using the traditional approaches to obtain clients, but nothing seemed to work in this high-net-worth community he was attempting to serve.

Tony recommended that this agent try a new tactic: approach growing his business from his heart rather than his head. At the time, there was a trash strike and it had gone on for a significant amount of time. Trash was piling up as a result. The unsightly trash along the streets was an eyesore—not only to potential residents, but also to the community that resided in the area.

Rather than ringing doorbells, making signs, or contacting the HOA of the neighborhood, this agent assessed the situation and took action. *There's trash on the ground. That's a problem. What can I do about it? Pick it up.* He went out and got a truck and trailer and began hauling off trash. He continued to do this for a few weeks, without any fanfare. He didn't tell the residents what he was going to do; he just did it. Residents started taking notice.

"Are you with the city?" they asked.

"No. I'm just a real estate agent. I care about this neighborhood and love to list and sell houses here. I hate to see it look like this. I just want to help until all of this gets sorted out."

The conversation ended there. He didn't go on to push his card on the person he was speaking with or leave flyers on the doorstep of every house whose trash he picked up. He just did the job. His actions were congruent with his values about service, as well as with his mindset about growth—he wanted to get more listings and to sell more houses. This was a good way to demonstrate that he cared about and was invested in the area, which was also true. Any guesses what happened next?

Word of mouth spread like wildfire. People in the neighborhood began telling their friends and neighbors about his efforts. He quickly became the real estate agent everyone was talking about and referring their business to. It's important to note that this guy didn't just pick up trash in front of his listings, or only on a specific street. He went all-in, house by house, and street by street, for weeks. He provided real value—surprising and emotional value—and people always gravitate to that.

If, in contrast, this agent focused solely on what made logical sense, he may not have been convinced to go all-in. Certainly not to the degree that he did. But sometimes that is precisely the point of leading with your heart and not logic. He didn't know that his cleanup—the value he was giving—would pay off the way it did. But his actions aligned with his values, so he couldn't help it. This is what it means to grow naturally. It's about authentically making a difference, solving problems, and making friends, one at a time.

If it sounds slightly confusing, think of it like this: though this real estate agent's original planned Impact was "to make sales," he led with his heart and just did what was right to impact the hearts and minds of the neighborhood. This Give was without promise of an outcome like a sale—he shifted his Impact to a bigger Impact: connecting to people's deeper values.

Follow your heart. Do the right thing. Lead with your values, and sometimes leave logic behind.

THE SEAMLESS VALUE PROPOSITION

Don't be afraid to look at your value proposition for additional potential. Stay attuned to the ongoing needs of your audience so you can refresh and innovate deep value they can connect to. This is exactly what Dropbox did to generate incredible growth by matching the needs of their core audience.

Top growth marketing expert Sean Ellis, author of *Hacking Growth*, shared the story with me on my podcast.[24] Sean described how his team put out a survey to their customer base with the specific goal of finding out which customers valued their service the most—their power users.

Finding these power users was not based on traditional metrics like size of business or number of users or number of logins. They ignored those metrics and instead looked for how much the users valued the service. They measured based on how much the businesses relied on Dropbox and how disrupted or upset they would be if they no longer had access to it.

The survey allowed Dropbox to identify a specific audience who could not live without it: those that weren't using the service so

---

[24]   Scott A. Martin, "Sean Ellis | Growth Hacking Mastery," October 18, 2020, in *Groundswell Origins*, podcast, 1:08:37, https://groundswell.libsyn.com /sean-ellis-hacking-growth.

much for file storage but for file *sharing*. This insight prompted Dropbox to *change its value proposition* and therefore its marketing, a decision that led to highly organic growth.

Patience at work looks like the Swan Effect. Natural growth is incremental, and leverages both creativity and common sense. It may feel slow, but it can be steady—a humble march in your chosen direction.

GROW INTELLIGENTLY

*"I don't need to do more smart things.
I just need to do fewer dumb things.
I need to avoid making emotional decisions and
swinging at bad pitches. I need to think!"*

—Keith J. Cunningham, *The Road Less Stupid:
Advice from the Chairman of the Board*

To be in business, you must have systems. To Grow, these systems must be running well—you've worked out all the bugs and hiccups, and natural growth is occurring. With this foundation in place, you can begin to scale. Eventually, this may mean adding lines of business, but the first step to intelligent growth is to make the most of what you already have.

To tap your full potential of Growth, you need to increase business from your existing audience: increase the number of individuals in your audience who buy from you and get more repeat business from those individuals, along with rapid, aggressive word-of-mouth referrals.

Each of these moments should be painless for your audience.

When it comes to buying from you, make it enjoyable and easy. Make your audience eager to come back because you're always innovating, and you make it dead simple to decide and spend. This is frictionless delivery.

When the experience of buying (and buying again) from you is so delightful and full of value, you can take the next step and empower your audience to tell others about you. This is seamless shareability.

FRICTIONLESS DELIVERY

*"Design is not just
what it looks like and feels like.
Design is how it works."*

—Steve Jobs

Frictionless delivery happens when each element of your system flows smoothly from beginning to end and results in your desired outcome. Don Peppers mentioned this in our discussion on the podcast:

The most important aspect of any customer experience is that it be as frictionless as possible. And that's why trustability is what I think of as one of the four qualities of a frictionless customer experience—along with reliability, relevance, and value.[25]

Whether this is an internal process or a front-facing interaction, it *all* affects your audience. Joe Pine offered some great advice about what those frictionless interactions should feel like for the customer:

> Satisfaction is not enough. You've got to reduce the sacrifices your customers are making. Understand them as individuals. Engage with them and figure out what they want. Whether it's collaboratively or some other method, figure out what they want. Then pull the actual good through the value chain to be able to produce [what] this individual wants at this moment in time.[26]

The good news is that once your process becomes frictionless, it requires fewer resources to maintain and increase growth. If you want to accelerate growth, start by increasing value and

[25] Scott A. Martin, "Don Peppers | Trust Is the New Currency." January 6, 2020, in *Groundswell Origins*, podcast, 1:03:00, https://groundswellorigins.com /podcast/don-peppers.

[26] Scott A. Martin, "Joe Pine | Rise of the Experience Economy," February 8, 2020, in *Groundswell Origins*, podcast, 1:01:02, https://groundswellorigins.com /podcast/joe-pine-2.

decreasing friction in your services. Stage experiences that have your audience immersed, captivated, and spending time because what you provide is unique and valued.

Put yourself in their shoes: where it is effortless for your customers to buy more, you need to spend more.

TIME WELL SPENT

What is the opposite of frictionless? Stickiness? Surprisingly, stickiness is not in conflict with being frictionless; it's how to hold attention, captivate, mesmerize, and create drama in your audience's mind. It is actually architecting experiences that have people value the time they spend with you on the things that matter. When things are seamless and everything just works, that can be a great service "experience," but having your audience feel the dramatic pull and desire to invest time and be in your environment is also a strategy to deploy—to *stage* an experience on top of service.

Like Kenny Rogers's famous line in "The Gambler," know when to hold your audience and when to walk away. You've just gotta know when it's right to make their interaction with you frictionless and easy and when to pull them into your experience so they view it as time well invested.

Be frictionless when it's a service and not frictionless when it's an experience. Think of it as a theme park. Paying your admission should be frictionless, but the experiences built on top of your service should by nature be captivating and immersive. Your audience wants into the park quickly so they can spend more time immersed in the experiences you have staged.

SEAMLESS SHAREABILITY

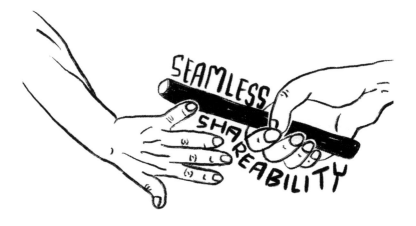

Word of mouth is one of the most powerful tools for growth. A certain amount of word of mouth will happen naturally as you serve your audience well. To go to the next level of exponential word of mouth, though, you need to ensure two things: that what people are sharing has value, and that the method for sharing it is easy.

People share when they feel like they are giving something of value to others—even if it's just a laugh from the latest viral meme—so creating value is always step one. If you don't deliver value, or the value you deliver has downsides, people are not going to share. (See the previous discussion of frictionless delivery, not to mention Build and Give.)

After you deliver amazing value, sharing comes down to one simple fact: people don't like to do things that are hard. Even if it benefits them, humans are more likely to avoid a negative experience than seek a positive one. How many promotions have been run where all a person needs to do is mail in a self-addressed stamped envelope and they will get back a free gift? Promotions like that are only cost-effective because most people don't care enough to put in the effort. Overcoming the obstacle of effort requires a payoff of extreme value.

The best thing you can do is make sharing easy. Make it effortless for your audience to pass on value to others, and maybe even receive value in return. If sharing is a hassle, your audience won't follow through with it, no matter how much they value the outcome. The only way to grow positive word of mouth exponentially is to make it *easy*.

Creating this system of seamless shareability will take some strategy and planning. Start by asking these questions:

- Is this valuable to my audience member?
- Is this something my audience member would share with other relevant individuals?
- How does my brand interact with my audience members?
- How does my audience prefer to interact with others?

- What are the barriers to sharing?
- How can we remove these barriers and make sharing effortless?

Next, think about timing. You have a limited amount of time to capture this shareability—at the height of the interaction when value is most felt, create an effortless way for your client to share their experience with someone else.

How can you design a process that equips them with what they need to pay their positive experience forward? This takes a little art and science. The art is in the design, visuals, relevance, and timing—the flow and experience. The experience of sharing can be beautifully designed. The science is in the offer, message, and mechanics—the functional components that fit together. The ideal is that it works, it's simple, and it makes sense.

For example, you might invite customers to share a discount code that offers significant savings, but you limit them to share that code with only one person. The offer is so appealing and com-pelling that it would be crazy for a customer *not* to share it and allow a friend to reap the benefits. In this case, if the code is of high enough value, your customer will do the targeting for you and forward it to the person they know will benefit the most. This puts you in contact with your next highly relevant prospect.

Systems are now in place to incentivize, track, and manage shareability. This has given rise to affiliate programs. These are performance-based programs in which you are rewarded for bringing customers into a program or offer. Affiliate marketing does work, but you are effectively paying people to promote you. That isn't necessarily a bad growth strategy—but it should only be a *part* of your strategy.

How deeply someone feels your brand helps them or adds value to their life is proportionate to how connected and valuable it *actually* is. Seems obvious, right? But before someone shares, they will inevitably ask, "What is in it for me?" Even when a person has a connection to your brand and sees the value, they can't help but double check that it directly benefits them to share.

And the complexity doesn't stop there. When a brand is already shared often by others, this may in fact prevent a customer from sharing. Part of what makes us human is feeling special. If you're overplaying, broadcasting, or removing a feeling that it is *special* to share, people likely won't. Think of the best-kept secrets—who doesn't want to be the hero that shares one of these? How can you incorporate your audience's desire to feel special and be a hero into your strategy of reasons to share your brand? Without a compelling case, people will only share if incentivized or on ad hoc.

However, there is one thing that compels people to share: when they have been transformed and/or the brand is deeply aligned with multiple values or their highest values. We call these people *raving fans.*

ALIGNMENT AS A GROWTH ACCELERATOR

The more connected to people's values, and the more valuable your brand is, the *more* people want to share. It's a critical consideration when estimating "shareability" or how much positive word of mouth your goods or service will create.

There is a chokehold that can be a challenge, and that is scale. When you're small, it's easy to be "the best-kept secret." Alternately, when your audience is compelled to share because your brand is aligned to their values, scaling is much less of a chokehold but still a consideration. The good news is that there is a solution.

Sometimes, making your brand shareable while also scaling is not about investing in more benefits (what's in it for your audience) or generating deeper connection or values (no matter how amazing that can be).

What is the sweetest sound a person can hear? Their own name.

The solution to scale is intimacy. With them. At scale. Personalize it.

Yes, find a way to make it more *personal!* The secret to getting around all of these needs as you scale? Personalization. How can your client put *themselves* into what you're sharing in a way that only adds value when *they personally* share it? Let them be the hero, be *seen* as the hero, and put their name all over it.

Here is a quick example. I ran a campaign with Fernie Wilderness Adventures, a backcountry snowcat operator, and they had very little visibility or traction in their nearby city, Calgary. We created a compelling headline—"Fernie's Deep White Secret"—and invited the owners and top sellers of every snow shop in the city to have a free day of powder on us. Total bucket list for most of these individuals. We appealed to the people who valued untracked powder above all else. We are talking fanatical individuals. This was so connected to their deep passion that they *all*, 100 percent, said yes. We had a photographer take photos of the entire day. We then shared on social media (tagging them) all the Hero photos, selected the best photo of each shop's staff, printed them as posters with the wording "Fernie's Best Kept Secret," and gave them their own *personalized* posters of their day.

Fernie Wilderness Adventures sold out the following year. They have never looked back. Their fans were compelled to talk about the experience, smells, sights, and sounds of that day (emotional priming), and the posters, which were personal and unique to each shop, shared the price of a day of riding (rational messaging). For years, those posters had prime real estate in the shops, visible and proudly being shared and talked about.

Just add personalization.

When you provide value, it's okay to ask for this reciprocity—and, in fact, seamless shareability becomes another way to Give to your audience. When they buy and buy in, they *want* to be a part of your Groundswell. So, invite them, delight them, and reward them with the gift of sharing value with others. We asked the snowboard shops to push and recommend the slower times/dates of the year, and it worked. We became shareability partners, frictionally.

While your frictionless execution may compel your audience to engage and commit for their own purposes, if you don't set your system up to create seamless shareability, you'll hijack your own potential growth.

TRUST IS FRAGILE

What happens when you make a mistake, and it gets broadcast and shared? It can have the complete opposite effect. How you handle this is critical to maintaining a positive outcome with sharing.

Mistakes happen—how do you fix yours? So many people have been burned, it can be hard to trust that a business will keep their word. What happens when you mess up? Are you really going to keep your promise? Good reviews are no longer enough. The cry for authenticity now requires you to put out a bit of your dirty laundry so people can see the truth. Owning your actions can help close the gap of trust that may have opened when it comes to public perception. It seems easier to ignore rather than face the difficult job of addressing problems head-on. But you are being graded by how responsive you are, the tone of the response, combined with the transparency of ownership of the problem.

Make some of your brand's problems public, along with a demonstration of how you helped solve those problems. The new real juice is in converting the disenchanted—or just being reasonable with the unreasonable. When people look at reviews, they are interested in seeing how you will respond. Too many good reviews, and they will think it's fake. Mistakes will happen—own them and ensure you have a process for rapidly responding appropriately.

A WORD ABOUT AUTOMATION

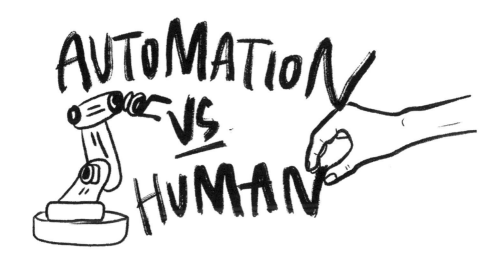

One way that many entrepreneurs pursue quick growth is by outsourcing and automating areas of their business as quickly as possible in anticipation of the growth to come. Automation is the most efficient way to scale a business in the short-term, but we don't just want to scale if that means sacrificing all the culture that's been built—and all the value that has been given—up to this point. Doing so would destroy the Groundswell and inhibit sustainability.

If you're not careful, automation can be harmful to your business.

Many businesses use automation for the sake of speed and efficiency, and put their focus on leads, marketing, publishing, and top-of-the-funnel activity. This approach vastly decreases the human component of your brand and inhibits the ways in which you can connect with your audience.

Dean Graziosi, a very successful entrepreneur with an incredible background in building success over the long term, shared this in an interview:

> ...too many people are trying to automate or outsource certain parts of your business. In today's world, outsource what you can, just never outsource your marketing. Never outsource your connection and the intimacy you create with your clients. That can never be outsourced. And we're all looking for the magical outsource company to do it, [but] every big company [that] I see grow has to do it themselves.[27]

Think of it this way: would you automate your interactions with your employees? Do you think doing so would make them feel more valued, or less valued? This same reasoning should apply to everyone you interact with, from prospects and clients to suppliers and employees.

---

[27] Scott A. Martin, "Dean Graziosi | The Art and Science of Marketing." February 19, 2020, in *Groundswell Origins*, podcast, 53:00, https://groundswellorigins .com/podcast/dean-graziosi.

You can't automate your way into a Groundswell. You have to roll up your sleeves and engage, especially when it comes to marketing. Don't allow impersonal barriers or overly curated marketing to come between you and a conversation with your audience—keep your intentions clear, your impact human, and your efforts connected. Brands that use automation to create more human interaction *increase* intimacy as they scale. These brands—the ones that really connect with their audience on a human level—are going to win in the long run.

*"Elegance is when the inside is as
beautiful as the outside."*

—Coco Chanel

When I think about growing elegantly, I think about ivy. Not the poisonous kind—the vigorous, woody, evergreen vine that contentedly climbs lattice and spreads across stone. English ivy, for example, is flexible, easy to propagate, and can grow up to one hundred feet in length. It is, quite simply, beautiful. Ivy is not frantic or messy. It's intentional and patient, steadily and elegantly earning its place. Let's not forget, the ivy plant has a bit of an attitude, an air of confidence. It is no coincidence that Ivy League schools are named after it. Cool. Confident. Elegant.

To be remembered, you must be memorable. You must adapt to changes and weave like ivy to be resourceful and natural in your growth. This is precisely the kind of growth that is sustainable. This is a form of elegance. Ever had an experience that was so seamless and smooth that it was memorable because of that alone? Because it was simply beautiful?

How can we be more like ivy? With simple complexity that does no harm.

Simply Complex

As Leonardo da Vinci put it, "Simplicity is the ultimate form of sophistication." There's nothing more elegant than a simple solution. We humans have a tendency to overcomplicate things. Simplicity is *not* loud and obnoxious. It's not an ad bursting with too many colors, ALL CAPS, random starbursts, and exclamation points after every sentence. Simplicity is *not* having a guy dressed up like a pickle waving a big sign while yelling, "Hey, hey, come on in!" No, this is not simple. And not at all elegant.

Simplicity is the DoubleTree giving you a warm cookie to welcome you when you check in. It could not be any less complex, but it's simply brilliant.

Focusing on restraint and aiming for ease of growth is essential to sustainability. This also includes the messaging, the branding, and the customer experience.

Some of the smartest growth marketers understand that it's about keeping things uber simple. Take Google. They have one thing: a search bar. A touch of class and a beautiful user experience will positively impact your audience's desire to interact, share, and commit to your business and its offerings, as well.

Give people exactly—and only—what they are looking for. As Joe Pine and James Gilmore wrote in *The Experience Economy*, "Fundamentally, customers do not want choice; they just want exactly what they want."

*"Our prime purpose in this life is to help others.
And if you can't help them, at least don't hurt them."*

—Dali Lama

When you're selling, you're creating a state of mind within your audience. There's responsibility in that.

Patient, confident, and giving…

There's an additional key element of Groundswell Growth that I want to highlight: natural, intelligent, and elegant growth must also do no harm. Harm can look like everything from interruptive marketing to forceful sales that make people feel pushed. Or the harm can be subtle, like a badly designed billboard that is out of place in either content or context. The pain can be low but it's there. For example, when a digital ad wrongly targets me with a makeup and perfume advertisement, it detracts from my experience and is out of place. Alternatively, people flock to watch the ads during the Superbowl and even replay them—they are so creative and innovative that the interruption is welcomed.

But there is another level: when the content that entices you to consider a call to action is viewed as value-added content. Remember the "waiting for waves" ad by Instinct? I saw this as content, not an advertisement, and the content in the magazine is all part of my desired experience because it is connected to something I value.

So, Growth needs to be a bit of *art* with the science—an elegant and simple solution that is connected to your audience. Create based on values and on what people value, and they will respond. We need to stop just chasing growth for growth's sake.

Don't sell out to sell.

This means not pursuing growth "at any cost." If growth makes you compromise your value and values, if it doesn't align your

Epic Center to your Epic Outcome, if it costs you the value-based culture you have built...then the price of growth is too high.

That kind of growth is the antithesis of a Groundswell.

Your brand is the promises you make, and to rise to a higher standard, you must look inward and be willing to adjust as necessary.

Everything that you put out into the world—from your culture to your goods and services to your ads and web copy—should align with your values and give value to others, even those who are not your audience. When you approach growth with your website or your ad, it should reflect your deeper brand promise.

A Groundswell Parable:
Choosing When and How to Grow

After the first big Give debacle, Koa and Kalani made sure
to have the infrastructure to support new clients needing
surf lessons. They integrated lessons with a walk-through of
their goods and options so there was also an opportunity to
bring sales into the experience. They got into a great rhythm
of giving and connecting with their value and values to their
audience. This led to natural growth, slow and steady, that
they could manage well. Like a vine, they were shaping it in
the direction they wanted as it grew.

Their success led to more chances for growth—faster growth.
Opportunities came a-knocking.

They had several investors reach out asking to distribute their
goods, franchise their shop, and license their brand.

Company A and Company B wanted to distribute their goods.
Company C was interested in franchising as well as a mass
distribution and brand licensing agreement.

But these opportunities didn't necessarily align with their values and vision. They didn't want to simply grow fast—they wanted to grow beautifully. Luckily, because they had cultivated patience and learned from their mistakes, they knew better this time around. They learned what really matters to them and their audience, and the kind of growth that feels good, not just looks good to an investor.

With this sustainable perspective, they are able to decide which avenues are authentic and aligned with their mission, goals, and Epic End, rather than just growing for growth's sake. Koa and Kalani decided to work with Company A, a heartfelt business owner, to open a second Groundswell Goods shop; and with Company B, a small string of shops, to distribute with. But they opted out of working with Company C for mass distribution, licensing, and franchising. It was a slower but more elegant approach and allowed them to maintain the intimate connections they cherish with their partners and fellow surfers.

PATIENCE IS THE NEW GROWTH HACK

PATIENCE IS STILL THE NEW GROWTH HACK

"Be not afraid of growing slowly, be afraid only of standing still."

—Chinese proverb

To grow sustainably, sometimes you have to put in the work even when there's no immediate evidence of result, reward, or response. You have to go on faith.

When I think about the natural path, I always think first about planting a seed. If you have a seed in your hand, you have more than a seed. You have the possibility of a plant, and that plant has the possibility of bearing fruit, which contains even more seeds. That's valuable.

When you plant the seed, you take all the possibility you've held in your hand and entrust it to an intuitive system and intentional process with the understanding of the impact that seed will make. When you don't see the seed sprout upon immediate insertion in the soil, do you shout at the dirt, "Hey, what are you doing? Where are my tomatoes?"

Of course not.

You wait. And more than that, you wait with confidence. Sure, you may throw a little fertilizer over the seed and adjust your drip line to water it more effectively. But, really, you're *seeing the vision* and *trusting the process*—and then you're waiting.

Your brand should be the same. You ease into the Growth process and do your due diligence: Build and Give. You may even get creative and broaden your garden by planting some peppers and onions in anticipation of all the ways you can leverage your tomatoes. You might build a lovely fence or trellis to complement your garden, and ensure you draw bees and butterflies. Then, when the time is right, what you've planted will grow.

"Great marketing only makes a bad product fail faster."

—David Ogilvy

Imagine a world in which marketing had more meaning. In which it transcended from eye pollution to art, performing a beautiful dance with branding and service. Imagine if marketing was a personalized, individualized, interactive experience.

Why not create that world today?

The most beautiful marketing is simple, frictionless, and useful. It not only looks lovely but also produces a beautifully communicative state. It not only works, but it feels good—to all parties.

You can entertain, educate, and inspire. And if you do all of this in a way that's memorable and no longer feels like marketing, it will still function to move commerce. There's a transaction happening, sure, but there's also beautiful synchronicity.

You know what you're doing and why. Your audience is never interrupted. Nothing is irrelevant. Everything is aligned with purpose—both yours and your audience's. All of this allows you to feel really connected to your good or service, and it allows your audience to feel really connected to their purchase. It's beautiful because it's intentional—aligned on so many levels.

Today, the feeling associated with marketing is often the opposite of beautiful. Instead, it's coercive, cluttered, and chaotic. Approaching your marketing as a beautiful interaction may require a big shift in your thinking and processes.

Instead of thinking of marketing as ads, think of it as *adds*. Ask yourself: Do your ads add value to anyone's life? Are they useful? Are they relevant? Do they have a pleasing aesthetic? Are they hurtful or helpful? Are they interruptive? If handled thoughtfully and consistently, these factors will set you apart from the competition.

Remember, you are not here to stick with the status quo. You are here to combine all of that inertia into a powerful Groundswell of change. View Growth through the lenses of intelligence, elegance, and nature, and add this to the guiding principles of Build and Give, and you will find your true and most beautiful potential.

From here, you can take your Groundswell to the next level, where Transformation changes everything.

We're not trying to find more people who can benefit us; we're trying to connect with *humans* we can benefit. When you show up generously from the beginning, the return lasts long after the first transaction.

TRANSFORM

BEYOND LOYALTY

"If you add the value, you will become the brand.
Find a way to add more value
than anyone else does."

—Tony Robbins

What if you could compel your *audience* to exponentially grow your brand?

What if you could build a growth loop powered by the loyalty of your audience? An engine that plants, nourishes, and harvests the attention and commitment of your audience. A self-sustaining ecosystem of value exchange. A dream scenario for a brand, right?

It's entirely possible. After all, exponential, sustainable, healthy Growth is what a Groundswell is all about. But to access this level of commitment from your audience, you must give them a value so compelling that they cannot help but reciprocate. This is the rub that can potentially make achieving this final phase of

Groundswelling so elusive and challenging. Even after you've Built, Given, and Grown your value and your audience, if not handled with care, relationships can fall back into being transactions.

Remember the airline miles example? Despite a solid Give (frequent flier miles), if the airline service doesn't carry great value and a great experience, their customers may feel trapped and unhappy in the relationship.

So how do we do it better? How do we create committed and loyal relationships?

In the Origins section of this book, I shared Don Peppers and Martha Rogers' seminal framework *Get, Grow, Keep* as my foundation for how to generate a Groundswell. Their final phase, Keep, focuses on customer retention—ways of spurring loyalty and keeping your audience connected to you. This remains the spirit of the final phase of a Groundswell, but on a deeper level. We're not talking about traditional loyalty programs or point systems. We're talking about an ongoing, nurturing connection that results in the granddaddy of value: Transformation.

WAVES OF IMPACT

"Marketers make things better by making change happen."

—Seth Godin, *This Is Marketing: You Can't Be Seen Until You Learn to See*

Transformation is the most valuable thing you can give to your audience. It's multilayered and complex. It's dynamic and requires their participation, and—when achieved—has exponential potential for you and for them. But Transformation is rarely a single moment or interaction. The exponential starts with the incremental.

Move

In *The History of Love*, author Nicole Krauss wrote, "The oldest emotion in the world may be that of being moved; but to describe it—just to name it—must have been like trying to catch something invisible."

This is the first stage of Transformation—to simply move someone. It doesn't matter how small. Think of the increments of any relationship: from stranger to acquaintance, acquaintance to friend, friend to core group. It's all energy moving in the direction of deeper connection. The same thing happens with your audience. Over time, these small movements add up and can tip into a larger commitment. But you must move people emotionally before you can move them actionably toward commitment.

So how are you moving your stakeholders? It could be easier than you think, like showing up and letting them know you exist. This moves them from stranger to acquaintance without any expectation of them. Perhaps next they notice your Give and lean in closer, close enough to relate to what you're building and want to learn more.

Any time you give value and demonstrate your values, you are seizing the opportunity to reach and move the people who align with you. Your true audience will respond. You may have to Give a few times in order to move them to the point of having a real interaction with you—and that's okay. The unseen wave of marketing potential is just a ripple at this stage, but the wave is coming.

Change

You've done it—you've moved your audience forward to the point that they are directly interacting with you. Now change becomes possible.

Here, you have the opportunity to deliver on your values and to demonstrate the truth of who you are. It changes everything. Before this, your audience member only had a hunch and a hope of who you are. But now, after connecting and interacting with you, they know. This experience takes them beyond mere feelings into a reality. This creates trust.

While Move generates an internal reaction, Change generates external action thanks to this added layer of trust. It could be as simple as someone changing brands from, say, a PC to now buying all Apple goods—but the end result is a tangible impact: they are literally changed in some way, even if it's just changing behavior or commitments to a new line of business.

A positive interaction creates positive change, building more trust. When your clients interact with you and your brand, it changes the way they see you and can even change the way they view the world and how they move through it. It's a powerful moment that can lead to a powerful word-of-mouth engine. When a friend asks for a recommendation, your clients will suggest your brand, citing the positive change they experienced with you.

This is where most marketers live: acting as agents of change, constantly looking to convert clients to their systems, goods, or services—and invisibly enlist them to help change other people's experiences. This is where most great companies work and succeed.

But we are not here for great. We are here for exceptional. We are here to make the previously unseen wave into a visible, endless tsunami composed of individuals who will never be the same again.

TRANSFORM

You may not be aiming to upend every practical aspect of your audience's lives, but Transformation is change at the deepest level. It has the power to impact your clients' entire human existence—body, mind, and spirit. Not only will they achieve the results they want, and not only will they refresh the way they think about themselves and what they are capable of, but they will also connect to something greater than themselves and amplify their belief in humanity.

There is a famous tagline by Billabong that said, "Only a Surfer Knows the Feeling." It embodies the idea that once you stand up on a wave, you know, feel, and act differently and will never be the same again. Tony Robbins often repeats a phrase at the closing of each of his live sessions, "Life will never be the same again," underscoring the experiences his audience has come to expect. The *expectation* of Transformation propels your brand beyond loyalty and into the realm of folklore. Yeah, I said it.

The greatest power comes when your audience experiences real and personal change that matters to them. This is the highest value you can give, and it leads to the ultimate value you can receive: when those changed individuals share their personal experience with others.

And when you deliver on a promise, when aspirational value becomes actual value, you tap into that irrational response mentioned earlier in "Connection is the New Cash." Transformation creates raving fans who can't stop—and won't stop—talking about you with everyone they meet.

Over time, the impact of word of mouth continues building, like a never-ending wave that you get to create.

Ultimately, Transformation is about fulfillment—changing a person's needs from unmet to met, from empty to full. Your value gives them an avenue to align more fully with their values. This process requires the deepest integrity and intention. It begins with how you fulfill your promises to your clients, which translates to how

fulfilled your clients are by your services, and, finally, to how fulfilled you are as an entrepreneur.

Creating a Groundswell goes beyond meeting needs and into the
work of fulfilling lives.

LEVELS OF IMPACT

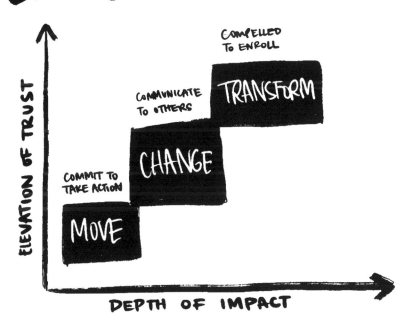

THE POWER OF AN EXPERIENCE

Digital analyst Brian Solis said, "Customer experience is the sum of all engagements and interactions a customer has with your business, in every step of their journey and lifestyle. It's what your customer feels, thinks, says (to you and others), and more so, what they do now and in the time to come that counts for everything."

Experiences can create stickiness and drama, seduction, and desire. Transformational experiences are moments in time when a person is irrevocably changed, inside and out, for the better. Creating this defining moment begins all the way back in Build and is carried through every phase that follows.

When all of that is in place, you then transform connection, trust, values, and exponential value into sustainability. Intentionally expressing your value and values across every facet of your business—goods, services, human resources, management meetings, customer service interactions, and of course, marketing—creates the atmosphere necessary for Transformation to take place.

Delivering a transformational experience can create much more impact than just top-line sales. Simply put, it can turn your customers into more customers. Put massive energy first and foremost into *retaining existing clients*, and you'll gain more output from them in return. The strategy of growth is the strategy of conserving energy—so it's not actually about *new* growth. The constant churn of acquiring more won't accomplish that.

TRANSFORMATIONS — GUIDE

EXPERIENCES — STAGE

SERVICES — DELIVER

GOODS — MAKE

COMMODITIES — EXTRACT

WELCOME TO THE TRANSFORMATION ECONOMY

There is a model known as the Progression of Economic Value, explored in Joe Pine and James Gilmore's pivotal book *The Experience Economy.*

This is what they have called an "economic theory of everything." The model starts with commodities being extracted, then made into *goods,* which are then customized by delivering *services.* Building on that, you can customize these services by staging *experiences,* and end in *staging experiences in a customized way for each individual by guiding them into the ultimateTransformation.*

Transformational experience gives each individual the one thing they want and what they need: a true impact that lasts. Creating this specific moment of lasting Transformation is the key to your success, your growth, and your sustainability of both.

This means that Growth is not a time to cut corners just to see the numbers increase. Rather, it's a time to double down the focus on your goods, services, and experiences. Growth—and Groundswell Growth, at that—comes from understanding that your customer experience is part of your good.

To give the most value possible, you need to be able to keep giving value reliably over time—not go crazy just so you can surge for a few years and then burn out. If at any point a deficit arises, it must be addressed at the root. This may mean returning to and retooling an earlier phase of the Groundswell framework. Remember, the phases never stop—they continually flow forward, rolling one into the next, building on each other. Together they reach the shore with wave after wave of Epic Impact.

How are you progressing the economic value you get from and *give to* your clients?

What about if you stage experiences, and in fact go beyond that, guiding your audience into *transformational* experiences? Joe Pine explains:

> You need to go from thinking about just goods and services to understanding that there are whole opportunities in providing more value. Go beyond experiences to transformations, where you're actually helping customers achieve their aspirations—such as healthcare in fitness centers, universities, and so forth. What we talked about early on, too, is going from understanding multiple customers in a market to understanding that, no, in fact, there are multiple markets in a customer. And if you get that, then everything else will follow, because in order to serve the multiple markets inside each customer,

you have to do everything that I talked about before. And that was a light bulb for me.[28]

Joe is talking about treating each human like an individual—treating each as the individual they are in the uniqueness of the moment, situation, and interaction. If you can give them an experience of change, you can deepen their trust and loyalty. You can help them transform who they are and make the world more beautiful for them. This Transformation is the hidden potential of untold growth.

The value progresses through each stage.

You extract grapes from the vine, and they are considered commodities (natural stuff). Then you could turn those grapes (goods) into wine (tangible things), which is something that is made or created from the commodities. Then you could ship the wine to people's homes (deliver services), which is an intangible activity but a progression from the goods.

---

[28] Scott A. Martin, "Joe Pine | Rise of the Experience Economy." February 8, 2020, in *Groundswell Origins*, podcast, 1:01:00, https://groundswellorigins.com /podcast/joe-pine.

Next could be a wine store or an event where you stage an experience that is personal and memorable, making this a distinct economic offering, "as distinct from services as services are from goods."

Last is where you change the essence of the experience into something profound for the audience or individual so that they are no longer the same. They are guided through a process of Transformation, like becoming a sommelier. You could imagine this being an educational guided tour of how grapes are made, tasted, and paired with other items so that the audience's opinion, consumption, and total point of view of consuming wine are changed forever.

Retention is the byproduct of passionate loyalty. It doesn't just happen; it is inspired by things we immensely value—specifically, moments of impact. Moments of impact happen through meaningful experiences.

TRANSFORMATION DESIGN

Just as adequate power and continued energy in the same direction of the storm are required to sustain the waves all the way to shore, a Groundswell requires heartfelt passion, a vision of impact, authenticity and originality, and the commitment to see it through. Together, these are the driving force—your Epic Center—to your Groundswell, as well as your Epic Outcome within the impact zone. Generating Transformation is **the means and the end** of a Groundswell.

- Anchor the name of the Transformation you want to see. (Groundswelling)
- Exquisitely detail the from-to process. (From Marketing to Groundswelling)
- Design the strategy in phases. (Build, Give, Grow, Transform)
- Embark on the stages within the Transformation. (Move, Change, Transform)
- Chart your course with ICE (Impact, Confidence, Ease) from your Epic Center to your Epic Outcome.
- Map how you will guide the experiences that you can individually customize to move your audience to change and ultimately Transform.
- Create captivating and personalized experiences that generate an Epic Outcome for each individual.
- Set sail on the never-ending journey of innovating elegant growth within the business, within yourself, and within your relationships.
- To guide you during those moments of doubt and stormy waters, look to the horizon and see the Epic Outcome and impact this will have. To keep the course, head straight toward Transformation.
- Uniquely and deliberately name the identity of the newly transformed individuals. (Swellpreneurs)

A Groundswell Parable:
Transformations One Step at a Time

Koa and Kalani's journey of building their audience started with architecting their Epic Center: to support their community and make surfing accessible to all. They built momentum by taking the time to design a scalable vision of the experiences they wanted to share, and they grew through connection and trust at every interaction. Koa and Kalani moved people to act and go surfing for the first time, and then to change their behavior to make surfing part of their lives, ultimately transforming them from regular people to people who call themselves surfers.

A transformation of identity.

THE SEA OF SAMENESS

Now that we have detailed the identity of the individuals who are transformed, there is a critical distinction in the approach to successfully compelling others to engage with your brand (the key to never-ending growth). If you build your Groundswell all the way to Transformation, the most potentially dangerous Epic Outcome is sameness.

If people feel that the Transformation is like a sausage factory where everyone has the same experience and becomes the same, this will not self-replicate and compel others to enroll. Transformation must, by design, be an individualized experience, and the name/identity should create an inner circle of others who see themselves as part of a new group where they all share in the understanding of the Transformation. The transformed people should also see themselves as having their own experience they can express and share; their unique story is so captivating because it's theirs—100 percent, authentically their own wave.

They have set a new standard for themselves to never be the same again—and they see the immense value in the journey so clearly that they onboard, grow, and challenge others to get the courage to bravely embark on *their* own individual journey.

Together, these individual transformed riders of the storm bring others and challenge them to paddle out to catch their own wave.

THE IMPACT ZONE

I hope it's clear by now that the key to sustainable growth is *not* chasing nonstop new connections. It's investing in every single connection you already have and demonstrating your commitment to *their* growth. Sustainability is not going wider with your audience, but deeper.

Your pursuit of deep connection is showcased in your audience's journey with you, when you deliver value and guide the Transformations. Your commitment to delivering value is not business as usual; it's exceptional, and it entices more with every interaction. As you consistently and intentionally serve your audience beyond their expectations, from your heart, you create bonds of trust.

This is the real magic for growth.

The more trust grows, the stronger the connections, and the more your audience opens up to new experiences, to deeper personal investments, and to more chances for you to demonstrate your value and commitment to them. This attentive care naturally and inevitably leads to more genuine connections and deeper relationships. This level of connection creates the ultimate potential for sustainable growth for your brand—trust that surpasses loyalty into lifestyle. You're now part of their tribe, and part of their fundamental beliefs and identity, just as they are a part of yours.

Already, you will have tapped into an ecosystem of value, but to tap the sustainable growth of a Groundswell requires that last and most powerful moment of impact: Transformation that your audience will not forget. As these experiences fulfill your audience's human needs at the deepest level, you build trust at an epic level. Beyond alliance and even allegiance, it's a transformation from *loyalty* to *love*. This is the unified wave of a Groundswell. When you give love—genuine care, wanting the highest best for every human you interact with—your impact is unstoppable. That's what we're chasing.

Now, driven by their newfound quality of life in the face of their transformative experience (and not by price, convenience, or even quality), these raving fanatics don't wait for someone to ask for a recommendation—they actively share with anyone who will listen.

That connected word-of-mouth (what clients say about you) *is* part of both your *impact* and sustainable growth.

What your customers say *is* your brand and the ultimate sustainable growth engine. The initial energy to create the Transformation doesn't end; in fact, it can be transferred to others. When people are transformed, they are compelled to share with others *and* committed to enrolling them—this is at the core of turning your existing audience into advocates inviting others to join the experience.

As you provide transformative experiences to your audience, you transform your sustainability—not only to continue existing and growing, but also to keep making the impact you care about most. Your impact zone is the focus, and it reaches as many people as possible.

This is where your Epic Center of Origin reaches your Epic Outcome. The proverbial waves of Build, Give, Grow, and Transform hit the reef, and all that energy transforms into a cresting wall of water that lands with an impact of meaningful experiences.

Your mission is to discover your brand's unique method for creating value, connection, and moments of Transformation for your audience. This is your key to generating *your* Groundswell of growth and sustainability.

THE FINAL WAVE

"The tides come in, and the tides go out—
but low or high, serene or tempestuous,
the sea is always full."

—Jaimal Yogis, *Saltwater Buddha:*
A Surfer's Quest to Find Zen on the Sea

It's a beautiful experience to build a brand that impacts the world. We have such precious little time on Earth to leave it better than when we rolled up. I have deep belief that nature, the universe, God brought you here to do something important—something that echoes into the future.

Now that you know how your efforts to Build, Give, Grow, and Transform become a sustainable growth loop for your brand, you can pursue your brand and the impact you desire to give with focused intention. As you do, you will see for yourself how to generate more output with less effort over time.

But don't get it twisted—this doesn't mean you've arrived.

None of the phases of Groundswell ever stop. You are always building, giving, growing, and sustaining transformative experiences. In fact, our goal is to keep a loop of Transformation. The cycle of innovation needs to be self-perpetuating so that you start again with Build, then Give, then Grow, and then Transform anew—even differently.

Lean into innovating. Re-Build. Find new ways to Give. Create even more elegant ways to Grow. Recognize that the Transformation journey *is* the never-ending wave that sustains you, allowing your brand to continuously impact new horizons of Epic Outcomes.

When you reach this point of transformative impact on your audience, you access the next level of Groundswell Growth: a never-ending wave. *A soliton.* As defined by Susan Casey, author of *The Wave: In Pursuit of the Rogues, Freaks, and Giants of the Ocean*, "a soliton is a solitary wave: a wave that behaves like a particle. Unlike a periodic wave, it is self-contained, and even in a collision with another soliton it will remain unscathed. It's the essence of coherence. Solitons are among the most powerful forces in the ocean."

A soliton is a wave that requires no new energy to be sustained. It becomes self-perpetuating, constantly creating an impact zone where the wave has the most power and force for good.

My goal—my purpose—is to become a Groundswell for good. To create an ocean of marketers and brands perpetually growing and influencing others to create a better and brighter future. Marketers have the power to be change agents, to promote the values that are meaningful to us down to our very soul.

As my mentor Tony Robbins said, "The only limit to your impact is your imagination and commitment." What is your commitment to imagineering your impact on the world? How far will you go to transform yourself, your good, and your organization so that you can then transform your audience? Are you willing to do the work and maintain your focus and energy to make sure your Groundswell hits the shore? Are you willing to be a leader with pure focus from your Epic Center to your Epic Outcome?

Because really, your Groundswell is one outcome: it's you and your journey—the reason deep down you started out in the first place. I want to invite you back to the beginning—to your point of origin. You aren't building a brand to sell widgets. You're here to transform lives and create impact. The feeling you're chasing, my friend, is fulfilment. What I like to call being "soulfully stoked."

Business offers us a spiritual journey and a potentially powerful way to impact the world around us, the people we serve, and the profits we produce. This journey is not the same for everyone, but it exists deep within each of us.

It's time for *you* to dive into the storm that kickstarts your Groundswell and discover the power of Transformation for yourself.

In fact, there is another wave you can tap that is considered the most powerful unseen wave. It's bigger, and it's a version of a soliton. It could be described as an "internal wave," which also exists in nature. Susan Casey defines it for us, too: "An internal wave is a soliton—a big one. As its name indicates, it's a wave that travels *within* the ocean rather than through it."

The final unseen wave of never-ending growth is you. These internal waves of self-reproducing energy are the core of your being, not doing.

Your Groundswell *is* going to move, change, and transform the world, but a more profound impact is your own Transformation. You are now a swellpreneur and part of an inner circle of maverick marketers, conscious creators, and impact entrepreneurs who are leveraging Groundswelling and transforming business as usual into business as beautiful.

Paddle out.

ACKNOWLEDGMENTS

The list of people I need to thank is extremely long. So many people along my journey of life and business have made an impression and impacted me in ways that led to this book.

First and foremost: my beautiful and patient wife Jill, who has tirelessly brought me food, quieted the dogs, and dealt with me being barricaded in my office while working on this project. She is my epicenter whom I affectionately call my "Jillyfish." She has been going with the flow with me on this project for almost three years. The truth is that she is my muse and the source of my energy. Her love and support have been critical to this book reaching its completion. I am deeply and eternally grateful I met you, Jillyfish, and that you agreed to jump on this adventure with me.

Secondly, my two best teachers: my parents who adopted me. When I really analyzed my journey of helping business with impact, I realized they were the OGs of impact in my world. They spent more than five years of their own time and money volunteering and giving back to others to make this world a better place. They have been such an example of how to live to a high ethical standard, and they've set the standard for our family.

My other teacher, Tony Robbins. From when I first met him in the pages of the book *Awaken the Giant Within* to being one of his Platinum Partners and getting direct training from him today, Tony has shaped my entire trajectory. His guidance has been critical to my success. Further, he is also the OG of Groundswell. The very essence of the transformation section (growth loop) I modelled was written after experiencing the results he created for his business ventures.

My two children, Davis and Anna: I am so deeply proud of you, now both part of Groundswell. I could not be more excited about your future and the extent to which you continue to work together. My children are my legacy, and I hope this book and the results of what we are building allows them to make an even bigger impact on the world. May they make a dent in the universe that will be a lot bigger than mine.

My extended family: over the years, you have been so gracious toward my focus on work and my missing so many events. My siblings, Norren, Karen and Dean: you all have been so supportive and understanding. The wolf pack specifically Kyle, Ben & Sophie I am so grateful to have you as family. All the Norris clan, so appreciative of how you have welcomed me into the family and support my work endeavors and this mission.

To my little brother, Mark: no words can express how much I

appreciate you. You have been—and always are—there for me, without any hesitation or judgement. You are such an incredible human who has taught me so much about how to live. Your partner, Cindy, also holds a special place in Jill's and my heart—we enjoy our beach fires together and making tequila mockingbirds, just the four of us on the island.

To all my podcast guests: you have given me so much content, and so many thoughts and ideas that have helped shape this book. Bruce Kasanoff, who wrote the forward and kicked off my first two season episodes, your insights and unique points of view have really set the tone for the book and Groundswell overall. Two of my biggest mentors, Joe Pine and Don Peppers, who are at the core of my strategies for building my career in marketing and who have influenced this book: thank you.

Michael Brenner, Jay Baer, Neil Patel, Dean Graziosi, JP Sears, Dave Navarro, Gina Bianchini, Lucas Digrassi, Joe Puuzzi, Cheri Cohen, Tucker Max, Tulsi Gabbard, Morgan Maassen, Ashley Faus, Randy Frish, Jacob Malthouse, Alec Stern, AJ Wilcox, Chris Do, Brian Fanzo, Robbie Kellman Baxter, Sean Ellis, Yousuf Bhaijee, Jeff Pensiero, Neil Schaffer, David Allison, Kristin Zhivago, Chris More, Jaiya and Ian Ferguson, Shaun Tomson, Geoffrey Moore, Gary Henderson, Pauline Brown, Master Co, David Meerman Scott, Tim Williams, Adam Doolittle, Katie Gertsch, Jeremy Miller, Sean Callagy, Shiny Unsal, Jeff Cochran, Gabor George Burt, Matt

Mosteller, Brittany Krystle, Blair Enns, Tim Hughes, Nikki Sharp, Dr. Elizabeth Lindsey, and one more amazing human…

Guru Singh: when we first dropped the Spiritual Groundswell episode, I had no idea what reverberations of impact it was going to have. Since then, we have spent countless hours working on The Mindful Marketer series, collaborating and co-creating a new way to explore building your business of impact. We would meet each week and film, and it brought me so much joy and insight. Without a doubt, having this time to learn from you has been its own spiritual journey. I deeply enjoy and love our continued friendship.

This project had some very significant contributors that I need to really highlight. First, Kimberly Kessler, who was my scribe. She was my tirelessly patient supporter, helping me through the process. She took the time to understand what I was trying to say and give this book life and shape when I didn't know how to write it on my own. Kimberly, I'm so deeply grateful to have had you working with me on this. And agreeing to experience a Tony Robbins event for book research. Total champ.

You will also notice the unique and original sketches in this book, all done by the incredibly talented and lovely Taylor Kinser. She really created the book I wanted to make. Taylor, without your visuals and design skills, it would not be what it is today.

Susan Casey, author of The Wave: I so appreciate your deep knowledge of waves you're giving me definitions and details that honestly created this book's much-needed ending. Your description of inner waves and solitons completed the book perfectly.

I would not have been in touch with Susan if it weren't for Dr. Elizabeth Lindsey, whom I have grown to deeply respect for the discussions around ancient wisdom, way-finding, and mindful marketing that have been so important to this work. Thank you for officially giving me the Hawaiian name Koa and for the context around how the Hawaiian traditions could be respected and interwoven into this book to help others.

Each of my clients over the years has been a testing ground for so many of these ideas, and I want to underscore a few that have had the most impact. First, Deb and Kim Serovic, whom I enjoyed a decade of catskiing and working with on their brand. They gave me license to try so many unconventional marketing techniques—especially at the dawn of social media. What a journey of growth. Mitch Hancock of Basecamp, who has become a close friend. We really started a brand that I am so proud of. Annieca Acker, who has been seriously one of the most fun personal brands to work with. Thanks to her, I started working with Andre Vicario and on his Mod Financial and Mod Jets brands; getting to know him, his lovely wife Kim, and his family has been a highlight of the last couple of years. To Craig Bundren, Matt Sadler, Leti and Kenji,

Master Co, Jamie Zografos, and so many others I have become friends with in the Tony Robbins ecosystem: what a joy it has been to work with you all.

Recently, I've been working with and launching Vertica Fitness with Katrina and Michael Wyckoff—a true Groundswell from the ground up. I cannot wait to see what happens next and have enjoyed the deep bond and friendship we have made.

This is what is amazing: I have become friends—meaningful friends—with nearly all the people I have had as clients and worked with. I have so many people who are left unmentioned, and some I don't even know at all, like José from American Airlines, who changed my life over thirty years ago by giving me a ticket home.

So many gifts and little things people have said… The books I have read and people I've learned from have contributed to this book. I want to, from the bottom of my heart, thank you all. You are the Groundswell origins that have resulted in this project and its impact on helping others transform business into waves of good.

ABOUT THE AUTHOR

Scott has spent over twenty-five years in digital, direct, social, and content production and marketing as an agency owner and strategist to national brands. He works with entrepreneurs and executives to launch sustainable growth marketing ecosystems. He constantly questions whether he's a business "growth hacker" or ambitiously lazy. Scott simply sees his role as finding ways to work smarter.

He has built a reputation for striking a middle ground between leading-edge marketing innovation and traditional, proven approaches. Simply put, Scott makes sensible, informed, forward-thinking decisions. Savvy marketers of national brands have hired him to directly develop a wide array of strategic marketing programs over the years.

Over the past five years, Scott has been recording *The Groundswell Origins Podcast*, where he shares insights from the top industry leaders to help marketers and entrepreneurs navigate the future and build sustainable programs that are positively impacting the world. His lineup on the podcast includes some of the most iconic names in the industry.

Learn how you can leverage Sustainable Growth Marketing by listening on iTunes: www.Groundswell.fm. Connect with the book resources @ www.Groundswelling.com and lastly join other swell-preneurs on their journey in the community called Groundswell Inner-Circle @ www.GroundswellinnerCircle.com

Made in the USA
Coppell, TX
16 March 2023

14296904R00215